GRAND CANYON
THE COMPLETE GUIDE

©2014 DESTINATION PRESS & ITS LICENSORS

ISBN: 978-0-9825172-6-0

Written & Photographed
by James Kaiser

Special thanks to AJ Lapré, Tom Pittenger, Lon Ayers, Dawn O'Sickey, Colleen Hyde, Pam Frazier, Tricia Lund, Ginger Reeve, Gray Thompson, Cat Zusky, Peter Brewitt, Peter Bohler, Brian Gootee, Clayton Norman, the Grand Canyon Association, and the entire staff at Grand Canyon National Park.

As always, special thanks to my family, friends, and all the wonderful people I encountered while working on this guide.

All information in this guide has been exhaustively researched, but names, phone numbers, and other details do change. If you encounter a change or mistake while using this guide, please send an email to changes@jameskaiser.com. Your input will help make future editions of this guide even better.

Additional Image Credits
Denver Public Library, Western History Collection, p.62:T#188
Grand Canyon National Park: p.42:#5281, p.43:#00133, p.56:#012, p.57:#445, p.60:#05423/08976, p.61:#008/09903, p.65:#11339, p.66:#16237, p.70:#14642b, p.73:#13868, p.76:#825, p.77(Bill Bass):#14718, p.75:#011, p.78:#02435, p.82, p.83:#17700, p.84:#01573, p.85:#30, p.167:#16950, p.125:#7448, p.126:#11822, p.127:#16251, p.144:#5972, p.157:#12084, p.160:#12005.
Wildlife Photos: p.46, p.48, p.49, p.50, p.51, p.52, p.53, p.54, p.55
Bureau of Reclamation: p.88, p.202, p.212, p.213
Earth Island Institute: p.89
North Wind Picture Archives: p.68, p.69, p.79, p.81, p.87
Peter Bohler: p.55, p.182, p.186, p.188, p.192, p.263, p.266
Printed in China

GRAND CANYON

THE COMPLETE GUIDE

5th Edition

WINNER
(1st Edition)

Benjamin Franklin Award
Best Full-Color Travel Guide

Independent Publisher Book Award
Best Travel Guide

FSC
www.fsc.org

MIX
Paper from
responsible sources
FSC® C005748

JAMES KAISER

CONGRATULATIONS!

IF YOU'VE PURCHASED this book, you're going to Grand Canyon. Perhaps you're already here. If so, you're at one of the most amazing places on earth—an act of geology so massive that it can be seen from space, and so beautiful that it lures over four million visitors each year.

My first introduction to Grand Canyon was in college, driving cross country on my way to California. When I reached Grand Canyon, I walked to the rim, basked in the view, and snapped a few photos. Then I climbed back into my car and headed to Las Vegas. Did I like the view? Of course. Did I realize that Grand Canyon had much more to offer? Not really.

It wasn't until several years later that I realized my mistake. In 2003 I went on my first Grand Canyon river trip. It was—and still is—one of the most incredible journeys I have ever taken. For three weeks I rafted down the Colorado, running rapids and hiking to dozens of spectacular sights— lush side canyons, hidden waterfalls, ancient Indian ruins. River guides, many of whom had spent *decades* rowing the Colorado, imparted their love and knowledge of the Canyon to me. By the end of the trip, I was hooked. I returned to Grand Canyon again and again, hiking the trails, studying the geology, and learning as much as I could about this amazing place.

Looking back, I can't believe I ever took Grand Canyon for granted. Sadly, many first-time visitors continue to make the same mistake. They step out of their cars, bask in the view, and then run off to their next destination. Vegas? Check. Hoover Dam? Check. Grand Canyon? Check. One of the most magnificent places on earth and they missed it!

That's where this book comes in. From hiking to river trips to scenic flights, Grand Canyon has it all. But it can be an incredibly overwhelming place. This book breaks it down, shows you the best that Grand Canyon has to offer, and equips you with everything you need to make the most of your time in the park. So go for a hike, drive along the rim, or spend the night at a historic lodge. But whatever you do, don't peek over the rim and wonder what to do next!

CONTENTS

The SOUTH RIM p.95

The most famous and popular part of Grand Canyon—home to nearly two dozen breathtaking viewpoints. Spend the night at a historic lodge, dine on a gourmet meal, or simply wander the rim and take in the world-class scenery.

The NORTH RIM p.253

Wild and remote, the North Rim combines stunning views with just one-tenth the crowds of the South Rim. Because of its cool, high elevation, the North Rim is covered in lush forests of spruce, fir, and aspen, giving it a feel more like the Rocky Mountains than the desert Southwest.

The COLORADO RIVER p.197

Often referred to as the Nile of America, the Colorado River flows free for 277 miles in Grand Canyon. Along the way it passes through a stunning landscape hidden from much of the outside world. Without question, a river trip through Grand Canyon is one of Earth's most amazing outdoor adventures.

HAVASU CANYON p.283

Part tropical paradise, part Southwestern dreamscape, Havasu Canyon is one of Grand Canyon's most amazing sights. The physical and spiritual home of the Havasupai tribe, Havasu Canyon is famous for its gorgeous turquoise river that tumbles over the canyon's red rocks in a series of stunning waterfalls. The only challenge is getting there.

INTRODUCTION

ONE MILE DEEP. Ten miles wide. Two hundred seventy seven miles long. Covering 1.2 million acres in northern Arizona, Grand Canyon is a breathtaking act of geology. Teddy Roosevelt called it "the one great sight every American should see." The panorama from the rim is one of the most impressive sights in the world, but Grand Canyon is much more than just a pretty view. Hidden within its depths are fascinating creatures, geologic marvels, the ruins of an ancient civilization, and some of the best outdoor adventures in North America.

Cut by the Colorado River over the past six million years, Grand Canyon is a colossal labyrinth of towering buttes and deep side canyons. Although massive, most visitors head to one of two developed areas: the South Rim or the North Rim. The South Rim, located two hours north of Phoenix, is by far the more accessible and popular of the two. Home to six of the park's eight lodges, it's what most people think of when they think of Grand Canyon. The North Rim is located just south of the Arizona/Utah border—one of the least densely populated regions in the United States. Its remote location means fewer crowds, but equally stunning views.

Hiking trails descend from both rims to the bottom of the Canyon. Along the way they pass though 11 layers of ancient rocks, ranging in age from 250 million to nearly two *billion* years old—almost half the age of the Earth! At the bottom of the Canyon, near the junction of three popular trails, lies Phantom Ranch, an overnight lodge offering comfortable beds and home-cooked meals. Guided mule trips are also offered along several Grand Canyon trails, and both day and overnight trips are available.

Twisting through the bottom of the Canyon is the Colorado River. Fed by Rocky Mountain snowmelt before slicing through the deserts of Utah and Arizona, the Colorado is the most impressive river in the West. Although currently plugged by dams along much of its length, the Colorado flows free in Grand Canyon, dropping 2,000 feet in 277 miles. Over 20,000 people embark on river trips through Grand Canyon each year. In addition to 60 thrilling rapids, river trips provide access to spectacular hiking trails, stunning Indian ruins, and gorgeous waterfalls. Without question, a river trip through Grand Canyon is one of Earth's most incredible outdoor adventures.

Bright Angel Trail

HIKING

GRAND CANYON OFFERS some of the best hiking in the Southwest. The range of scenery in the park is incredible, from cool pine forests to narrow slot canyons to everything in between. There are trails that skirt the edge of the rim and trails that plunge thousands of feet to the Colorado River. And don't forget the Canyon's two billion years of amazing geology—arranged chronologically for your viewing pleasure.

Sound too good to be true? Not at all. But before you hit the trail, there are some important things that you need to know. First, there are two types of hikes in Grand Canyon: day hikes and backcountry (overnight) hikes. Day hikes are very straightforward—just pick a hike and go. Backcountry hikes, however, require a bit more planning. Due to the large number of visitors interested in backcountry hiking, the National Park Service limits the total number of backcountry hikers allowed on each trail to reduce crowding and maintain the wilderness experience. Backcountry hikers must apply for permits, which are granted on a first-come, first-served basis.

Second, unlike most places on the planet, many of Grand Canyon's trails start at the top and end at the bottom. This "mountain-in-reverse" style of hiking poses several unique challenges. For starters, a hike into the Canyon seems deceptively easy on the way down. Each year park rangers rescue hundreds of hikers who overestimate their hiking ability and become stranded near the bottom of the Canyon. In general, it takes about twice as long to hike *up* to the rim as it takes to hike *down* to the Colorado River. Another factor is temperature—the lower you go, the hotter it gets, with temperatures up to 20°F hotter at the bottom of the Canyon. Despite these challenges, hiking in Grand Canyon is a fantastic experience. Just follow the rules and tips on the following pages and your trip will be safe and enjoyable.

If hiking in Grand Canyon still seems a bit intimidating, the Grand Canyon Field Institute (GCFI) offers a variety of excellent backpacks, day hikes, and rim walks led by knowledgeable, experienced guides. The GCFI, which works in partnership with the National Park Service, is dedicated to enhancing understanding and enjoyment of Grand Canyon through firsthand experience. Their outdoor activities accommodate a wide range of ages and abilities. For more information visit www.grandcanyon.org/fieldinstitute.

Day Hikes

There are two types of day hikes in Grand Canyon: day hikes along the rim and day hikes that descend partway down the Canyon along Inner Canyon trails. The North Rim has the most day hikes along the rim, with about half a dozen popular trails. The South Rim only has one day hike along the rim: the 12-mile Rim Trail, which is paved most of the way and passes by many of the South Rim's most popular viewpoints. The South Rim also offers access to several popular Inner Canyon trails that can be followed partway down as a day hike. If you do plan on dayhiking into the Canyon, however, know your limits and give yourself plenty of time to return before sundown.

Backcountry Hikes

If you're thirsting for more than a quick day hike, Grand Canyon offers a number of spectacular backcountry hikes that start at the rim and descend into the Canyon. These hikes, best tackled over multiple days, are called backcountry hikes because they follow trails that pass through terrain classified by the park as "backcountry." The park service has divided the backcountry into four management zones: Corridor, Threshold, Primitive, and Wild.

Corridor Zone trails are well-maintained and equipped with modern facilities. There are three Corridor Zone trails in Grand Canyon: the Bright Angel Trail (p.168), South Kaibab Trail (p.178), and North Kaibab Trail (p.274). Not surprisingly, these trails are the most popular backcountry hikes in the park. Because Corridor Zone trails are heavily trafficked and provide relatively easy access to water, Backcountry Rangers strongly recommend that first-time Grand Canyon backcountry hikers stick to these trails.

The Threshold Zone offers trails that are officially unmaintained but generally in fair condition. There are two Threshold Zone trails covered in this book: the Hermit Trail (p.184) and the Grandview Trail (p.190).

The final two management zones, Primitive and Wild, cover extremely rugged terrain beyond the abilities of most Grand Canyon visitors. Considerable Grand Canyon hiking experience is necessary in Primitive and Wild zones.

To camp in the backcountry, you must apply for a permit from the park's Backcountry Office. Be aware that the backcountry is divided into "Use Areas" delineated on commercial maps. Knowing which Use Area a trail traverses is necessary when applying for a backcountry permit. Also note that camping in the Corridor, Hermit, Monument, Horseshoe Mesa, and Tapeats Use Areas is limited to designated campsites or campgrounds, and camping there is limited to two nights per hike. (From Nov. 15 to Feb. 28, however, you can camp up to four nights in popular Corridor campgrounds.)

Trail Conditions

Before you go hiking, be sure to check the most up-to-date trail conditions at www.nps.gov/grca/planyourvisit/trail-closures.htm. This handy website lists all current closures, hazards and other important info.

Backcountry Permits

Permits are required for all overnight backcountry hikes in Grand Canyon. Each year the park service receives about 30,000 requests for about 13,000 available permits. Although these numbers seem intimidating, if you plan in advance a permit isn't too hard to come by. On short notice, however, a backcountry permit can be difficult to obtain, especially during peak hiking season in March, April, May and October.

Backcountry permits are issued by the Backcountry Reservation Office. The South Rim Backcountry Office, located behind Maswik Lodge, is open daily 8am–noon and 1–5pm. The North Rim Backcountry Office, located in the Administrative Building, is open the same hours mid-May to mid-October.

The earliest a permit can be requested is on the first day of the month, four months prior to the proposed start date. In other words, if you want to apply for a permit sometime in June—June 1, June 15, June 30, etc.—the earliest you can apply is February 1. The backcountry permit request form is available on Grand Canyon's website (www.nps.gov/grca). As of this writing, only written permit requests are accepted, but a new online reservation system is in the works! (Check the park website for the latest regarding online reservations.) For detailed information on the backcountry permit process visit Grand Canyon's website or call the Backcountry Office: 928-638-7875 Monday–Friday, 1 pm–5 pm Mountain Standard Time.

Although most people request permits well ahead of time, the park service does offer a very limited number of last minute permits along Corridor Trails. To obtain a last minute permit, head to the Backcountry Office as soon as you arrive and request a number. Numbers are called out the next morning at 8am, and if your number isn't called you will advance to the top of the list for the following day. The process is then repeated. Thus, if you request a number several days in advance, there's a good chance you will obtain a last minute permit.

Permit Cost

There is a non-refundable $10 fee per permit, plus $5 per person per night below the rim ($5 per group above the rim). Permit cancellations are subject to a $10 cancellation fee. Frequent hikers can purchase a one-year Frequent Hiker membership for $25 that waives the initial $10 fee for each permit. If a permit is cancelled three days or more before the start date, the $5 per person fee can be applied to a future hike.

Hiking Tips

DON'T HIKE TO THE COLORADO RIVER AND BACK IN A SINGLE DAY

Each year the park service rescues hundreds of day hikers stranded in the Canyon. Hiking to the river and back seems deceptively easy on the way down, and by the time a weary hiker realizes how difficult the hike up will be, it's often too late. Evacuations are time consuming and costly. (Helicopter evacuations can cost a stranded hiker upwards of $3,000 per flight.) By planning ahead and understanding the trail, you can easily avoid a needless evacuation.

BRING PLENTY OF WATER

The biggest dangers on the trail are not scorpions, rattlesnakes, or mountain lions—in fact, these animals pose relatively little threat. The biggest killers are dehydration, heat exhaustion, and heat stroke. Rangers recommend drinking one gallon of water per day in the summer. Drink small amounts often, even if you don't feel thirsty. By the time you feel thirsty, you're already dehydrated. Some trails have access to water, but many do not. Ask about a trail's water availability before you start hiking, and filter or purify all water from springs, creeks, etc.

USE EXTREME CAUTION WHEN HIKING IN THE SUMMER

In the sweltering summer months, heat-related dangers—dehydration, heat exhaustion, heat stroke—become even more pronounced. Temperatures rise as you descend into the Canyon. The average temperature at the Colorado River is roughly 20°F higher than the temperature along the rim. The best ways to stay safe are to avoid hiking during the middle of the day and to drink plenty of water.

MAKE WAY FOR MULES

Mules have the right of way on all trails. If you encounter mules, step off the trail on the uphill side and follow the directions of the mule wrangler.

BRING PLENTY OF FOOD

Just as important as drinking is eating. Salty snacks replace electrolytes that the body loses through sweating. If you drink water but don't replace electrolytes, you run the risk of developing hyponatremia, which can lead to seizures and sometimes death. When hiking in the Canyon, eat more than you normally do, and eat small amounts often. Every time you drink, you should also eat.

CHECK BACKCOUNTRY CONDITIONS ONLINE

The park's official website (www.nps.gov/grca) has a "Backcountry Updates and Closures" page that offers current information about backcountry conditions.

FLASH & DEBRIS FLOODS FLOWS

FLASH FLOODS ARE one of Grand Canyon's greatest dangers. Although dry for much of the year, heavy rains pound Grand Canyon in late summer. During monsoon season—July, August, and early September—thunderstorms sweep through the region on an almost daily basis, sometimes dumping several inches of rain in a few hours. The rocky, sun-baked landscape and sparse vegetation do little to absorb the water or slow it down. Runoff from these storms is channeled into side canyons, and if the rain is heavy and the side canyon drains a large area, a flash flood can form. Flash floods race through side canyons at speeds topping 23 feet per second, often pushing forward a wall of water several feet high. The force of a flood is so powerful that it compresses the air in front, sending pebbles and small rocks flying through the air in advance of the approaching wall of water.

Even more frightening, flash floods can form when skies are clear and sunny overhead. Storms in the region tend to be highly localized, dumping several inches of rain over a concentrated area while land just a few miles away remains dry. In the late summer of 1997, 12 tourists were hiking through Antelope Canyon (not far from Grand Canyon) when a thunderstorm 10 miles distant dumped an inch and a half of rain in less than an hour. The runoff from this storm gathered with astonishing speed, sending an 11-foot wall of water roaring through Antelope Canyon that killed all but one of the hikers. The sole survivor had been pressed against the canyon wall, gasping for air as the flood raged past. By the time the water subsided, every stitch of clothing on his body except his boots had been ripped off by the muddy, gritty water.

Similar to flash floods, but even more destructive, are debris flows. Unlike flash floods, which are 80–90 percent water, debris flows are a deadly slurry of water, rocks, and debris—up to 60 percent solid material by volume. Roaring through side canyons at speeds up to 25 feet per second (three feet per second *faster* than flash floods), debris flows rip out trees and wash away boulders weighing hundreds of tons. On average, two debris flows are triggered in the Grand Canyon each year. Although few people have ever witnessed a debris flow, the resulting vibration shakes the ground for miles.

MULE RIDES

For over a century, mule rides have been one of Grand Canyon's most popular activities. Everyone from Teddy Roosevelt to The Brady Bunch has descended the Canyon on mule, and while hardcore hikers would never dream of passing up a chance to hike into the Canyon, for many people mules are the only way to go. These sure-footed animals are fun, convenient, and offer a genuine taste of the Old West. (And did I mention that they do most of the hard work for you?)

Although less demanding than hiking, mule riding is still a physical activity. Riders must sit up straight on a moving animal for extended periods of time, which requires more endurance than you might think. And then there's the fear factor. Mules are incredibly safe animals, but they often walk terrifyingly close to the edge of the trail. Sometimes it seems like they're doing this intentionally just to taunt you with their amazing sense of balance. In other words, mule riding is not for the faint of heart. But despite a few mild challenges, most people have no problems riding mules, and many consider the experience to be great fun.

The South Rim offers both day and overnight mule trips. Day trips head east of Yaki Point along the new East Rim Trail. Overnight trips follow the Bright Angel Trail to the bottom of the Canyon, where riders spend the night at Phantom Ranch, a small lodge offering beds and home-cooked meals. Riders return the next morning via the South Kaibab Trail. Two-night trips are also available. Reservations for South Rim mule trips are accepted up to a year in advance, and they are highly recommended during the busy summer months. The North Rim only offers day trips, including trips along the rim and trips that descend partway down the North Kaibab Trail.

No experience is necessary for a mule trip, but riders must be at least 4 feet 7 inches tall (1.38 m), speak fluent English so the mule can understand commands, and weigh less than 225 pounds (102 kg) for day trips along the South Rim and less than 200 pounds (91 kg) for overnight trips to Phantom Ranch.

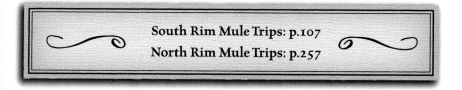

South Rim Mule Trips: p.107
North Rim Mule Trips: p.257

Colorado River Trips

A RIVER TRIP through Grand Canyon is one of Earth's most amazing outdoor adventures. Venture down the Colorado and you'll be treated to wild rapids, gorgeous sandy beaches, and some of the most stunning natural scenery in North America. The view from the rim is incredible, but the view from the river is beyond belief.

Over a dozen commercial outfitters are licensed to offer guided river trips through Grand Canyon. Overnight trips generally range in length from seven to eighteen days, and cost around $300 to $350 per person per day. The best trips are the multi-day adventures run between Lees Ferry (river mile 0) and Diamond Creek (river mile 226). One- to three-day "sampler" trips run at either end of the Canyon don't even come close to the scenery found in the heart of the park. Some companies also offer trips geared to specific interests such as hiking, photography, or natural history. But due to the immense popularity of all river trips and the limited number of passengers the national park service allows on the river each year, many trips are booked up to a year in advance.

Commercial outfitters run trips with both motorized and non-motorized boats. Motorized boats speed through the Canyon, allowing you to visit more sights in less time. While some people find this convenient, others dislike the whirlwind pace. Non-motorized boats come in two varieties: inflatable rafts and dories. Inflatable rafts cushion the impact of the rapids, resulting in a smoother ride. Rigid dories, piloted by skilled boatmen, offer a more tumultuous ride where flipping is a distinct possibility. But flipping is generally rare, and for many thrill seekers, elegant dory boats are the only way to go.

River-running season in Grand Canyon generally lasts from mid-April through early November. Summer is the most popular season, but it's also the worst time to go due to heavy crowds and scorching temperatures. The best time for a river trip is in the spring or the fall, when temperatures are mild and the river is much less crowded. Private, noncommercial river trips are also allowed, with private permits granted by lottery each year.

For more on running the Colorado River through Grand Canyon, see the Colorado River chapter (p.197).

RIVER OUTFITTERS

Aramark-Wilderness River Adventures
(800-992-8022, www.riveradventures.com)

Arizona Raft Adventures
(800-786-7238 www.azraft.com)

Arizona River Runners
(800-477-7238, www.raftarizona.com)

Canyon Explorations/Expeditions
(800-654-0723, www.canyonexplorations.com)

Canyoneers
(800-525-0924, www.canyoneers.com)

Colorado River and Trail Expeditions
(800-253-7328, www.crateinc.com)

Grand Canyon Discovery, Inc
(800-786-7238, www.grandcanyondiscovery.com)

Grand Canyon Expeditions Company
(800-544-2691, www.gcex.com)

Grand Canyon Whitewater
(800-343-3121, www.grandcanyonwhitewater.com)

Hatch River Expeditions
(800-856-8966, www.hatchriverexpeditions.com)

Moki Mac River Expeditions
(800-284-7280, www.mokimac.com)

O.A.R.S./Grand Canyon Dories
(800-346-6277, www.oars.com)

Outdoors Unlimited
(800-637-7238, www.outdoorsunlimited.com)

Tour West
(800-453-9107, www.twriver.com)

Western River Expeditions
(866-904-1160, www.westernriver.com)

Wilderness River Adventures
(800-992-8022, www.riveradventures.com)

CHOOSE YOUR
VESSEL

INFLATABLE RAFT

Oar-powered rafts offer a great mix of safety and excitement. Their flexibility allows them to bounce off obstacles and absorb much of a rapid's energy, resulting in a smoother ride. Tipping is rarely a problem, but expect to get wet. Some outfitters allow passengers to help paddle rafts.

DORY

These sturdy boats require the most skill to maneuver, and they provide the most thrilling ride in Grand Canyon. Made of wood or fiberglass, dories ride like a roller coaster, and they are more prone to flipping over than rafts. But for romantics, purists, and adrenaline junkies, these elegant boats are the only way to go.

J-RIG

These large, mortorized rafts are the fastest, most stable craft on the river. Carrying up to 20 people, they transport the majority of commercial passengers through Grand Canyon. Although J-Rigs visit more places in less time than non-motorized craft, some people prefer viewing one of Earth's greatest natural wonders at a slower pace.

Scenic Flights

No MATTER HOW much time you've spent peering over the rim of Grand Canyon, nothing can prepare you for the perspective you'll gain from the air. Viewed from above, the colossal maze of temples and buttes stretches all the way to the horizon, revealing some of the Canyon's most remote scenery.

More than 100,000 scenic flights soar over Grand Canyon each year. Grand Canyon Airport in Tusayan—the small town located a few miles south of the South Rim's main entrance—offers both airplane and helicopter flights. The main difference is the speed and the elevation at which they fly. Air-safety regulations require airplanes to fly roughly 1,000 feet higher than helicopters. Most people prefer helicopter flights, which provide a slower ride and a closer view, but airplane flights allow you to cover more ground in less time—and for less money. Depending on the route, helicopter flights last 25–45 minutes, while airplane flights last 45–90 minutes. Airplane flights generally cost $150–$200; helicopter flights generally cost $200–$280. (Discounts for children are often available.)

To reduce noise pollution, strict regulations limit which parts of the park scenic flights can explore. All told, over 75 percent of the park is off limits, including the air space above popular viewpoints on the North and South Rims and the "corridor zone" between them. Furthermore, no aircraft are allowed below the rim within the boundaries of the park. Despite these restrictions, scenic flights still reveal some of the Canyon's most beautiful scenery, most of which would remain hidden unless viewed from the air.

HELICOPTER FLIGHTS

Grand Canyon Helicopters (800-541-4537, www.grandcanyonhelicoptersaz.com)
Maverick Helicopters (866-689-8687, www.maverickhelicopter.com)
Papillon (800-528-2418, www.papillon.com)

AIRPLANE FLIGHTS

Grand Canyon Airlines (866-235-9422, www.grandcanyonairlines.com)
Papillon (800-528-2418, www.papillon.com)

National Canyon

GEOLOGY

GRAND CANYON IS a geological wonderland. There are few locations on the planet with so many eye-popping rock formations on display in a single place. It's safe to say that, had they been located elsewhere, many of these individual rock formations would be world-famous landmarks on their own. But within the depths of the Canyon they occur by the dozen. Rainbow-splashed mesas, temples, and buttes cascade down from the rim, extending for miles in either direction. Visually, there is so much to see—so many colors, textures, and shadows—that your sense of perspective often melts away. The scope of the scenery is dizzying, which is what makes staring out into Grand Canyon so much fun.

Even if you know nothing about geology, Grand Canyon is still an impressive sight. But take the time to learn about the forces that created it, and you'll look upon the Canyon with a fresh set of eyes. Suddenly, what was once amazing will become astounding. What once took your breath away will make your head spin.

On a human timescale, Grand Canyon seems ancient, peaceful, and serene. On a geologic timescale, however, it is young, violent, and exciting. Geologists were shocked to discover that Grand Canyon was created in less than six million years. When you consider that the Earth is over four *billion* years old, six million years seems like the blink of an eye. It's as if northern Arizona suddenly just cracked open and—*bam*!—there was Grand Canyon.

In reality, northern Arizona was sliced open by the Colorado River. After tumbling down from the Rockies, the Colorado twists and turns through the desert Southwest, picking up an enormous amount of sediment along the way. This sediment—a mixture of gravel, silt and clay eroded from the region's soft rocks—scrapes along the bottom of the river like sandpaper. During massive floods, when 100-ton boulders are tumbled like ice cubes, the rate of erosion accelerates exponentially. All told, the river has cut downward at a rate of about 6.5 inches every 1,000 years.

Over the past six million years, the Colorado has sliced through northern Arizona like a knife through a wedding cake. In the process, it has exposed dozens of layers of progressively older rocks, giving Grand Canyon one of its most defining characteristics: it is one of the few places in the world where you can view almost two billion years of Earth history just by glancing up and down.

ANCIENT ROCKS

MOST ROCKS IN Grand Canyon are sedimentary rocks, which form when sediments such as sand, silt, or mud gather in thick layers that, over time, are compressed into rock. Grand Canyon's sedimentary rock layers accumulated over millions of years on the prehistoric surface of northern Arizona, which has been home to giant sand dunes, muddy river deltas, and shallow tropical seas over the past 500 million years. These environments formed as ancient continents drifted across the globe and ancient oceans advanced and retreated over those continents. Eventually, eroded sediments from each of these environments formed distinct layers of sedimentary rocks. Sand dunes were cemented into sandstone, mud was compressed into shale, and the discarded shells of marine animals were cemented together into limestone.

Because Grand Canyon's rocks were laid down chronologically, one on top of another, they reflect a geological relationship known as *superposition*. Simply put, superposition means that the rocks above are younger than the rocks below. Move your eyes from the rim to the river and you are essentially staring back into time. At the bottom of the Canyon you'll find the region's oldest exposed rocks: Vishnu Schist and Zoroaster Granite. These rocks, referred to as the Precambrian Rocks of the Inner Gorge, are the only common rocks in Grand Canyon that are not sedimentary. Vishnu Schist is a metamorphic rock that formed roughly 1.7 billion years ago when intense heat and pressure transformed previously formed shale into schist. About 200 million years later, magma shot up into cracks in the schist and cooled into beautiful veins of pink Zoroaster Granite.

It wasn't until about 550 million years ago that the Tapeats Sandstone, the oldest major sedimentary rock in Grand Canyon, started to form. What happened in the one billion years between the formation of the Vishnu Schist is a bit of a mystery. During that time, up to 12,000 feet of additional rocks formed on top of the Vishnu Schist. But by 570 million years ago those additional rocks had eroded away, leaving an enormous gap in the geologic record. Geologists refer to such a gap as an *unconformity*. In Grand Canyon, the gap between the Vishnu Schist and the Tapeats Sandstone is known as the Great Unconformity—a name given by the early explorer John Wesley Powell. After the formation of the Tapeats Sandstone, additional sedimentary rock layers continued to accumulate. The youngest sedimentary rock in Grand Canyon is the 260 million year-old Kaibab Limestone, familiar to anyone who has walked along the South Rim.

Another rock formation found in Grand Canyon is the Grand Canyon Supergroup. These rocks started out as sedimentary rocks around one billion years ago, but they were later metamorphosed by heat and pressure. Today rocks from the Grand Canyon Supergroup are only visible from a handful of locations in Grand Canyon, such as Lipan Point on the South Rim.

The thought grew in my mind that the canyons of this region would be a Book of Revelations in the rock-leaved Bible of geology. The thought fructified and I determined to read the book.

—John Wesley Powell

ROCK LAYERS

KAIBAB LIMESTONE
Time of formation: 260 million years ago

TOROWEAP FORMATION
Time of formation: 262 million years ago

COCONINO SANDSTONE
Time of formation: 265 million years ago

HERMIT SHALE
Time of formation: 270 million years ago

SUPAI GROUP
Time of formation: 270-320 million years ago

GREAT
UNCONFORMITY

Ancient Landscapes Revealed

Grand Canyon's 11 major rock layers offer a rare glimpse into the ancient landscapes of northern Arizona, which generally looked nothing like the present landscape. Roughly 340 million years ago, the region lay under a shallow tropical sea similar to today's Caribbean. Over thousands of years, the shells of dead sea creatures piled up on the seafloor, and over time they were compressed into Redwall Limestone. Although limestone is often white, Redwall Limestone has been stained red by minerals seeping down from the Supai Group above. The rocks of the Supai Group formed about 300 million years ago, when eroded debris from the ancestral Appalachian Mountains washed over northern Arizona. (At the time the Appalachian Mountains were over 30,000 feet high, similar to today's Himalayas.) About 35 million years later, northern Arizona was home to a vast desert similar to today's Sahara. Giant sand dunes covered the desert, and over time they were compressed into Coconino Sandstone. Today you can still make out the slopes of sand dunes in parts of the Coconino Sandstone, as well as the fossilized tracks of reptiles that once prowled the ancient desert.

REDWALL LIMESTONE
Time of formation: 340 million years ago

TEMPLE BUTTE LIMESTONE
Time of formation: 370 million years ago

MUAV LIMESTONE
Time of formation: 530 million years ago

BRIGHT ANGEL SHALE
Time of formation: 540 million years ago

TAPEATS SANDSTONE
Time of formation: 550 million years ago

VISHNU SCHIST
Time of formation: 1.7–1.5 billion years ago

THE COLORADO PLATEAU

The sediments that formed the sedimentary rocks in Grand Canyon generally accumulated near sea level. So how did they end up thousands of feet *above* sea level? The answer has to do with Grand Canyon's location on the southwestern edge of a huge area known as the Colorado Plateau. At 130,000 square miles, the Colorado Plateau is the second largest plateau in the world after the Tibetan Plateau. It covers much of the Four Corners region and is filled with some of the most stunning natural features in America.

Starting around 60 million years ago, forces within the earth began pushing up the Colorado Plateau. By about five million years ago, it had risen over a vertical mile. The higher elevation led to increased precipitation, which led to increased erosion that stripped away many of the region's rocks. During this time, several thousand feet of overlying rocks were removed above the Kaibab Limestone, the top-most rock layer in Grand Canyon today.

As erosion chipped away at the Four Corners region, it sculpted one of the most dramatic landscapes in the world. But aside from their physical beauty, the sedimentary rocks of the Colorado Plateau are notable because they are so exquisitely preserved. This is due to the relative stability (geologically speaking) of the Colorado Plateau. As continents have drifted across the globe over the past 600 million years, they have smashed into one another like bumper cars, twisting and deforming their landscapes in the process. But the Colorado Plateau has somehow been sheltered from much of this action. As a result, its sedimentary layers remain relatively intact. By contrast, the rock layers in the geologically active regions surrounding the Colorado Plateau, such as the Great Basin and Rocky Mountains, have been severely deformed.

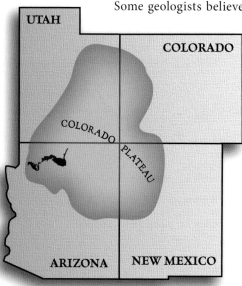

Some geologists believe the Colorado Plateau has resisted deformation so successfully because the earth's crust is relatively thick in the Four Corners region. In places, the crust beneath the Colorado Plateau is up to 25 miles thick. The crust of the Great Basin Desert, by comparison, is only 16 miles thick. So rather than buckle and break as it was pushed upward, the Colorado Plateau has remained relatively unaltered as a single tectonic block.

The uplift of the Colorado Plateau continues today. By some

estimates, it has risen as much as 1,000 feet over the past one million years. During this time, there have been some notable geologic hiccups along its boundaries. In western Grand Canyon, which lies near the boundary of the Colorado Plateau and the Great Basin, the earth's crust is thinner and more broken. As a result, hundreds of volcanoes have erupted near western Grand Canyon over the past two million years. At least 150 eruptions have sent lava pouring over the rim of the Canyon and tumbling down to the Colorado River. When the lava cooled, it often formed massive dams that backed up the river for miles. The largest dam, called Prospect Dam, was over 2,300 feet high. It created a massive reservoir that took 22 years to fill and stretched all the way to Moab, Utah. But in as little as 20,000 years, the gritty Colorado had completely eroded Prospect Dam.

THE COLORADO RIVER

MORE THAN ANYTHING, the Colorado River is responsible for the creation of Grand Canyon. But that's only part of the story. The specifics are considerably more complex. Early geologists, starting with John Wesley Powell, assumed that the modern river has always flowed along its present course. The way they saw it, the river cut down into northern Arizona as the Colorado Plateau rose up around it.

Then, in the 1930s and '40s, geologists came to the startling conclusion that the Colorado has not always followed its present course. Although the ancestral Colorado did flow into northern Arizona, passing through the region that would one day become eastern Grand Canyon, it avoided western Grand Canyon entirely. Rather than flow west through Arizona, it flowed *north* into Utah!

This led to a frustrating dilemma: if the early Colorado avoided western Grand Canyon entirely, how did western Grand Canyon form? That question has yet to be answered definitively. Much of the evidence has long since eroded away, so facts are hard to come by. But some geologists have pieced together a general theory. Back when the ancestral Colorado flowed north into Utah, a second "lower" Colorado River originated somewhere west of Grand Canyon. Over time, the headwaters of the lower Colorado eroded east until they reached the western edge of the Colorado Plateau. As they continued to carve away at the landscape, the headwaters came closer and closer to the upper Colorado. Then, around five million years ago, a critical divide was breached between the two rivers. The lower Colorado captured the upper Colorado, and the upper Colorado started flowing west. At that moment, the modern Colorado was born.

For the next five million years, the modern Colorado River cut down into the landscape as the Colorado Plateau rose up around it—pretty much the way early geologists had envisioned it. But the river's rate of downward cutting has not been constant. The rate of erosion has varied considerably depending on which rocks the river has cut through. Soft sedimentary rocks (such as sandstone and shale) were cut through relatively quickly, while harder sedimentary rocks (such as limestone) took much longer.

Despite the varying rates of erosion, the Colorado cut through all of the sedimentary rocks in a remarkably short period of time. By about 3.8 million years ago, Grand Canyon was within 500 feet of its current depth. At that point the river was grinding through Vishnu Schist, the hardest rock in the Canyon, and its rate of downward cutting slowed significantly. Meanwhile, another characteristic of the river started to change. As the Colorado ground down the steep obstacles that once choked the river, its grade began to level out. Rivers with gentle grades are much less erosive than rivers with steep grades, so the Colorado's rate of downward cutting was further reduced. Over the past one million years, the river has cut down less than 50 feet.

This shocking fact reveals a tremendous amount about the creation of Grand Canyon. While the Colorado sliced into northern Arizona like a band saw between three and five million years ago, it has done relatively little since then. Contrary to popular belief, erosion in Grand Canyon does not occur at a steady rate. Rather, it happens in brief spurts when powerful forces pound away at the landscape. Periods of intense erosion almost always correspond to periods when massive obstacles—lava dams, the uplift of the Colorado Plateau—block an easy path for the river. The Colorado doesn't just find the path of least resistance. It creates it. This fact gives one pause when considering the ultimate fate of the man-made dams that hold back the river today.

THE CANYON GROWS

ALTHOUGH THE COLORADO River is remarkably good at cutting down, it barely makes a dent horizontally. In fact, the river often adds inches to the riverbank by depositing sediment. Yet in places Grand Canyon is over 10 miles wide. What's going on?

Although the Colorado carved out a remarkably deep channel, the width of Grand Canyon is mostly due to runoff from the rim. In both cases the mechanics are similar—gritty water grinds down the region's soft rocks, breaking them down into sediment that's flushed out of the Canyon. As runoff from Grand Canyon's rim flows down to the Colorado River, it erodes the Canyon's steep walls along the way. In effect, the Colorado's deep channel serves as a giant template, funneling much of the surrounding runoff into the Canyon.

But the rate of erosion along Grand Canyon's walls has not been constant. The walls of the North Rim have eroded up to 10 times faster than the walls of the South Rim. This has nothing to do with the rocks that are being eroded—both rims share the same rocks—but rather the amount of precipitation that tumbles down from each rim. Both sides of Grand Canyon are tilted slightly to the south. As a result, precipitation that falls on the North Rim runs *into* the Canyon, while precipitation that falls on the South Rim runs *away* from the Canyon. Because the North Rim receives much more runoff, its walls have eroded at a significantly faster rate—a fact readily apparent to anyone who has visited both sides of the Canyon. Viewed from the South Rim, the walls of the North Rim gradually recede into the distance. But viewed from the North Rim, the walls of the South Rim are steep and dramatic.

Despite their different slopes, both rims cascade down to the Colorado River in a series of craggy temples and buttes. This is also due to variable rates of erosion. Just as the Colorado has cut down through the Canyon's rocks at different rates, the same rocks have eroded horizontally at different rates as well. Soft rocks erode easily to form gentle slopes, while hard rocks resist erosion to form steep cliffs. This stairstep formation of rock layers is one of the defining characteristics of Grand Canyon. To frequent hikers, the familiar slopes and cliffs provide a constant reminder of one's depth in the Canyon.

Grand Canyon is also famous for its deep side canyons, which often form along faults where the land has lifted or subsided, creating a narrow channel where runoff accumulates. Over hundreds of thousands of years, the runoff carves out a deep side canyon in a self-reinforcing process. The larger the side canyon becomes, the more runoff it collects. The more runoff it collects, the larger the side canyon becomes.

Although flowing water causes most erosion in Grand Canyon, other forces are also at work. Frost wedging occurs when water freezes and expands in the cracks of rocks, producing massive pressures—up to 20,000 pounds per *square inch*—that split the rocks apart. In some cases, frost wedging triggers rockfalls that send massive chunks of the Canyon tumbling down to the river. Rockfalls also occur when soft rocks erode beneath hard rocks, creating a pronounced overhang that ultimately collapses under its own weight. This process is referred to as *slab failure*. In Grand Canyon, with its many alternate layers of hard and soft rocks, slab failure is quite common, and it's the reason why many of the Canyon's hard rock layers erode to form steep cliffs.

In the end, the creation of Grand Canyon was due to many factors. Rock formation, erosion, and tectonic forces all conspired to create the stunning landscape now on display. Millions of years from now, those same forces will have rendered Grand Canyon completely unrecognizable to modern eyes. So consider yourself lucky. You're alive for that brief moment (geologically speaking) when you can enjoy one of earth's most amazing natural features.

Want to learn more about Grand Canyon geology? Check out the Yavapai Museum (p.115) or a Geology ranger talk (p.107, 257)

Blooming Agave

ECOLOGY

MORE SUBTLE THAN Grand Canyon's geology, but equally fascinating, is the park's ecology. First-time visitors often assume the Canyon is barren and lifeless. In fact, this is anything but the case. Over 6,000 feet of sudden elevation change creates a stunning range of life zones lying remarkably close to one another. Nowhere is this more apparent than the North Kaibab Trail, which starts in the cool boreal forest of the North Rim and ends up in the scorching desert at the bottom of the Canyon. In a matter of hours, hikers pass by spruce trees and cacti, the equivalent of traveling from Canada to Mexico in a single day.

All told, Grand Canyon is home to 17 fish, 47 reptiles, 89 mammals, and 355 bird species. There are also over 1,750 plant species in Grand Canyon—more than in any other national park. The wide range of biodiversity in Grand Canyon is due, more than anything else, to temperature and precipitation, both of which are affected by elevation. Generally speaking, temperatures rise and aridity increases as you descend into the Canyon. From the rim to the river, the contrast between environments is often extreme. At the sweltering bottom of western Grand Canyon, an average of six inches of rain falls a year, and only rugged desert plants such as cacti and yucca can survive. The cool, high plateaus of the North Rim, however, generally receive over 30 inches of precipitation a year, supporting dense forests of spruce, fir, and aspen.

The Canyon's wide range of climates also affects the distribution of animals. Cold-blooded reptiles that thrive in the warm Inner Canyon are much less common on the rim, and rim dwellers that require a steady source of water are poorly adapted to much of the Inner Canyon. Animals are also affected by the distribution of plants. Because plants form the foundation of a healthy food chain, they play a vital role in determining which animals can live where.

But plants are also dependent on animals. Consider the relationship between the pinyon pine and the pinyon jay, a pale blue bird found throughout the Colorado Plateau. Pinyon pines produce large seeds too heavy to be dispersed by the wind. But the seeds are a staple of the pinyon jay's diet. After gathering the nuts, the bird buries them for later use. Some seeds are inevitably forgotten, however, and forgotten seeds often grow into new trees. Thus, pinyon pines provide the jays with an important source of food, and the pinyon jays ensure a healthy population of pinyon pines, creating a wonderfully symbiotic relationship.

When viewed as a whole, the plants and animals of a particular area form unique, interdependent communities called "biotic communities." From tropical rainforests to Arctic tundra, biotic communities are found in every environment in the world. In Grand Canyon, there are six major biotic communities: boreal forests, ponderosa forests, pinyon-juniper woodland, desert scrub, and the lush riparian habitat along the banks of the Colorado River. With the exception of the riparian habitat, these biotic communities generally form horizontal bands across Grand Canyon.

Because elevation has such a profound effect on climate, it seems reasonable to assume that the location of biotic communities could be based on elevation. Although elevation provides a rough approximation of where certain biotic communities might occur, many local environmental factors also come into play. Furthermore, many plants and animals live in more than one biotic community. In Grand Canyon, where a large number of biotic communities are packed tightly together, their boundaries become even more blurred.

Biotic communities are also affected by microclimates—small pockets of temperature and moisture that vary dramatically from their immediate surroundings. Microclimates are caused by a variety of environmental factors including local topography, proximity to water, and exposure to sunlight. South-facing slopes, for example, receive much more sunlight than north-facing slopes, making them significantly warmer and drier, even at higher elevations. This explains why desert plants such as yucca are found at high elevations on the south-facing North Rim, while shady pockets along the South Rim support small populations of Douglas-fir, a tree that generally avoids the South Rim's warmer, drier climate.

C. HART MERRIAM

The concept of biotic communities, or "life zones," where specific groups of plants and animals interact, was first developed at Grand Canyon by the biologist C. Hart Merriam. In 1889 Merriam, then director of the U.S. Biological Survey (and a founding member of the National Geographic Society), led an expedition to Grand Canyon to study the region's plants and animals. As he descended into the Canyon, he noticed distinct communities of plants and animals living together. He called these communities "life zones," and theorized that their location was due to the varying temperatures. Additional research would show that life zones are dependant on much more than temperature, but Merriam's Grand Canyon expedition was the first time plants and animals were studied living together in a quantifiable way. His groundbreaking work helped pave the way for the modern study of ecology.

GRAND CANYON WEATHER

Because Grand Canyon is located in the arid Southwest, it receives much less precipitation than most parts of the country. Although precipitation is minimal, it arrives in a fairly predictable pattern, falling in the winter and the summer in a nearly 50/50 split.

In the summer, prevailing winds arrive from the south, carrying moisture from the Gulf of California. As moist air passes over Arizona, it's lifted up and over the highlands just south of Grand Canyon, arriving at the Canyon cool and condensed. In the morning, when the sun heats the Inner Canyon, hot air rises and collides with the cool, moist air above. This sudden collision creates short-lived afternoon thunderstorms. In July, August and early September (a period referred to as "monsoon season"), these storms pound Grand Canyon on an almost daily basis.

SUMMER

WINTER

In the winter, prevailing winds arrive from the west or northwest, bringing moist air from the Pacific Ocean. The vast majority of this moisture is wrung out by the Sierra Nevada Mountains, but some does find its way into northern Arizona. Although winter storms in Grand Canyon are much less intense than summer storms, they often linger for days.

In the spring and the fall, Grand Canyon becomes extremely arid, resulting in dramatic temperature swings. Dry air allows up to 90 percent of solar radiation to reach the ground during the day. At night, however, the situation is reversed, and 90 percent of the Canyon's accumulated heat radiates back into the atmosphere through clear, dry skies. In humid areas, by contrast, only 40 percent of solar radiation reaches the ground during the day, but that heat is often reflected back by an insulating cloud cover at night.

ICE AGE
in
Grand Canyon

Twenty thousand years ago, near the peak of the last Ice Age, Grand Canyon was a very different place. Although the topography was nearly identical, the distribution of plants and animals would be unrecognizable to modern eyes. In the depths of the Ice Age, a cool, wet climate descended over the Southwest, forcing many plants and animals to retreat to lower, warmer elevations. Juniper trees, which currently grow on the South Rim, grew along the banks of the Colorado River during the Ice Age, and Douglas-fir, a tree currently found only in the park's highest elevations, grew on the Tonto Platform, 3,000 feet below the rim.

Many strange and wonderful creatures also roamed the region during this time, including mammoths, camels, and Merriam's teratorn, a bird with a wing-span more than 12 *feet* across. Grand Canyon was also home to the Shasta ground sloth, a massive animal that stood six feet tall and weighed over 300 pounds. But around 10,000 years ago many of these large animals went extinct, most likely due to overhunting by early human settlers.

As the glaciers that covered much of North America retreated between 15,000 and 10,000 years ago, the Ice Age drew to a close. In the Southwest, temperatures rose, the climate dried out, and plants and animals living in the Inner Canyon began a slow migration towards the rim. By about 8,500 years ago the inner canyon had been transformed from a woodland to a desert. The remarkable flexibility of Grand Canyon's plants and animals—retreating to the Canyon's depths when temperatures drop, climbing back to the rim when temperatures rise—is a powerful reminder that the park's seemingly fixed life zones are, in fact, highly dynamic and adaptable.

Air currents also affect microclimates. During the day, as the sun beats down on the region, hot air rises up the Canyon walls. At night, by contrast, cool air flows down from the rim. These invisible rivers of air, flowing up and down the Canyon's walls, allow a wide range of plants to survive in unlikely places in Grand Canyon.

Life zone boundaries are often blurred by Grand Canyon's dramatic topography, but the Canyon also acts as a formidable barrier to plant and animal movement. Consider the Abert squirrel, a small grayish squirrel that is entirely dependent on ponderosa pines as a source of food. During the last Ice Age, when the climate was much cooler and wetter, ponderosa forests stretched across much of northern Arizona, including the Inner Canyon. For thousands of years, Abert squirrels roamed throughout the ponderosa forests in the Inner Canyon, but when temperatures started to rise around 10,000 years ago, the ponderosa pines retreated to higher elevations. Trees growing in the depths of the Canyon moved up to the rims, and with them came the Abert squirrels. Some squirrels retreated to the South Rim; others retreated to the North Rim, creating two distinct Abert squirrel populations on either side of the Canyon. Over time, the squirrels living on the North Rim developed unique physical characteristics (most notably a striking white tail) that have led scientists to classify them as an entirely separate subspecies called the Kaibab squirrel.

The interaction between plants, animals, and landscapes is incredibly complex in any environment. But in Grand Canyon, one of the most dynamic environments in the world, this complexity is elevated further. At times, it can be overwhelming. Even seasoned naturalists sometimes find themselves struggling to comprehend the sophisticated ecology of the park. But Grand Canyon also presents a tremendous opportunity for study and exploration. You could easily spend a lifetime learning about Grand Canyon's ecology, which is what keeps many people coming back year after year.

An Unexplored Wonderland

Grand Canyon's vast, rocky depths are filled with thousands of caves, but only a small fraction of them have ever been explored. In caves that have been studied, researchers have found evidence of extinct Ice Age animals like the Shasta ground sloth, which stood six feet tall and weighed over 300 pounds, and Merriam's teratorn, a bird with a wingspan 12 feet across. Although Grand Canyon's massive size and inhospitable terrain have hindered extensive exploration, the region's arid environment is ideal for the long-term preservation of bones and other animal remains. With so much of Grand Canyon still unexplored, who knows what other fascinating discoveries lie waiting in the depths of the Canyon?

HUMAN IMPACT

THE ARRIVAL OF early human settlers from Asia coincided with the extinction of many large mammals such as horses, camels and sloths that once roamed Grand Canyon. Whether this "Ice Age Extinction" was due to overhunting or previously unknown diseases arriving in North America remains a mystery. But once it was over, Grand Canyon's distribution of plants and animals remained relatively stable for thousands of years. In recent years, however, Grand Canyon has experienced many subtle—and not so subtle—changes.

The most notable change has been to the Colorado River. For thousands of years, the Colorado flowed free above Grand Canyon. Melting snow in the Rocky Mountains unleashed annual spring floods, and by winter the river's volume had slowed to a trickle. The temperature of the silty water also varied dramatically throughout the year. Over tens of thousands of years, a handful of fish evolved to survive in these unusual conditions. All told, eight fish species are native to Grand Canyon, and six of those species are endemic to the Colorado River Basin (found nowhere else in the world).

In 1963 Glen Canyon Dam was built just upstream of Grand Canyon. Almost overnight, the river's downstream ecology was completely altered. Instead of spring floods and winter trickles, the river now had a consistent, steady flow. And because the dam-released water was drawn from the dark, chilly depths of Lake Powell, it entered the Canyon silt-free and numbingly cold. The cold, clear water provided terrific habitat for non-native fish like trout that were introduced for sport, and since 1958 two dozen non-native fish species have been reported in Grand Canyon. But the introduction of non-native fish has been disastrous for native species. Non-native species compete with native fish for food and, in some cases, prey on native fish directly. To date, three native fish species have disappeared entirely from Grand Canyon, and two, the humpback chub and razorback sucker, are struggling to survive.

The humpback chub first appeared three to five million years ago. Because it evolved in swift muddy waters, it developed some remarkable biological adaptations. Large fins allow it to easily maneuver rapids, small eyes protect it from silt, and when swift water passes over its pronounced hump, the chub is forced down

Humpback Chub

* Historic Range

toward the bottom of the river where the current is less strong, helping it stay put during floods. Humpback chub thrived in the virgin Colorado, but its population in Grand Canyon plummeted after the completion of Glen Canyon Dam. Although humpback chub can survive in the cold, dam-released water, they need warm water to spawn. In 1967 the humpback chub was declared an endangered species, and today only a few thousand chub survive in Grand Canyon. Most of them live at the confluence of the Colorado River and the free-flowing Little Colorado River.

In 2009 the National Park Service began relocating juvenile humpback chub from the Little Colorado River to Shinumo Creek, a small tributary of the Colorado further downstream. A waterfall in Shinumo Creek prevents non-native species from entering the creek's upper reaches, thus providing a safe haven for the young chub. The establishment of a satellite population of humpback chub is critical for the long term success of the species. A hazardous materials spill in the Little Colorado River, for example, might otherwise prove disastrous. Although the relocation program is still in its infancy, initial results appear encouraging.

Dramatic changes in the Colorado River post-Glen Canyon dam have also affected the riverbank. Massive spring floods used to roar through Grand Canyon, scouring the riverbank and preventing many plants from taking root. Over the past several decades, however, the dam's steady, consistent releases have eliminated large floods, and a dense thicket of shrubs and trees has sprouted up alongside the river. (Although the presence of these plants is technically unnatural, they currently provide valuable habitat for the southwestern willow flycatcher, which is listed as an endangered species.)

Among the riverbank's new arrivals is tamarisk, a plant native to the Middle East that was brought to America as an ornamental in the late 1800s. Tamarisk is remarkably resilient, and it has spread like wildfire along rivers throughout the Southwest, arriving in Grand Canyon in the 1920s. In addition to muscling out native plants, tamarisk trees suck up vast amounts of water—up to 250 gallons *per day*. In 2000 the park service began cutting down tamarisk, and to date roughly 270,000 trees have been removed from the park. In 2001 the tamarisk leaf beetle, which feeds specifically on tamarisk, was intentionally released in the West, and by 2009 the beetle had made its way into Grand Canyon.

Non-native species have also affected Grand Canyon's vast rocky spaces. When miners abandoned their search for Grand Canyon riches in the late 1800s, they often left pack animals behind. Burros, originally from the deserts of Africa, were rugged enough to survive on their own, and soon they were breeding and multiplying. By the 1970s there were as many as 350 feral burros living in Grand Canyon. Conservation groups grew alarmed that the burros were competing with native bighorn sheep for scarce resources, and the burros were rounded up one by one and transported out of the Canyon by helicopter. Many feral burro populations remain throughout the Southwest, however, and in recent years there have been reports of new feral burro populations in western Grand Canyon.

Mountain Lions &
KAIBAB DEER

Uncle Jim Owens

In 1906 President Theodore Roosevelt established the Grand Canyon Game Reserve on the forested Kaibab Plateau just north of Grand Canyon. James Owens, who became known as "Uncle Jim," was appointed manager of the reserve, and from 1906 to 1918 he claimed to have shot over 600 mountain lions there. The walls of his cabin were covered with mountain lion claws, and a sign outside advertised, "Lions Caught to Order, Reasonable Rates." At the time, mountain lions were considered vicious "varmints" with an insatiable appetite for wild deer and local ranchers' cattle. Exterminating such ruthless predators was considered both logical and necessary.

Between 1906 and 1924, however, the number of deer on the Kaibab Plateau exploded from 4,000 to 100,000. The deer soon outstripped the plateau's food supply, and over the next two years 60,000 deer died of starvation. Biologists concluded that the rapid rise and fall of the deer population was caused by the systematic reduction of mountain lions, which preyed upon deer and, it was argued, kept their population in check. The "Kaibab Deer Incident" became a fixture in biology textbooks, demonstrating how man's interference with nature can upset its delicate balance. The story of the Kaibab deer was referenced in both Aldo Leopold's *A Sand Country Almanac* and Rachel Carson's *Silent Spring*, two of the most influential environmental books of the 20th century.

Then, in 1970, the biologist Graeme Caughley challenged the basic assumptions of the Kaibab Deer Incident. He questioned the deer population data, which was determined largely through guesswork, and concluded that mountain lions played a relatively small role in regulating the deer population. Caughley argued that habitat changes caused by climate, ranching, and government policy had a far greater impact on the deer population than mountain lions. His conclusions gained wide acceptance, and references to the Kaibab Deer Incident were soon removed from many textbooks.

In recent years, however, Caughley's study has been challenged by biologists who believe that mountain lions *did* play a significant role in regulating the Kaibab deer population. The Great Kaibab Deer Debate, it seems, is far from over. Perhaps the ultimate lesson is that the natural world is often far more dynamic and complex than it appears at first glance. Despite all we have learned, our scientific understanding of nature is far from complete, and there is much that remains to be discovered.

Gooseberryleaf Globemallow
Sphaeralcea grossulariifolia

Mojave Aster
Xylorhiza tortifolio

Palmer's Penstemon
Penstemon palmeri

Cardinal Monkeyflower
Mimulus cardinalis

Desert Four O'Clock
Mirabilis multiflora

Mariposa Lily
Calochortus flexuosus

Prince's Plume
Stanleya pinnata

Grizzly Bear Prickly Pear
Opuntia polyacantha

Evening Primrose
Oenothera pallida

Brown-Spined Prickly Pear
Opuntia phaeacantha

Desert columbine
Aquilegia desertorum

Silverleaf Nightshade
Solanum elaeagnifolium

CALIFORNIA CONDOR

Gymnogyps californianus

With a wingspan over nine feet across, California condors are the largest land birds in North America. To see a condor in flight is a highlight of any trip to Grand Canyon, but for decades these magnificent birds were completely absent from the park. Thirty years ago, California condors sat at the brink of extinction with a worldwide population of just 22 birds. But thanks to a long-shot recovery effort initiated by biologists in the early 1980s, California condors are now making a remarkable comeback.

Although cursed with a face that only a mother could love, condors are extremely graceful in flight. Riding thermals, they can fly for hours without ever flapping their wings. Condors can reach top speeds of 50 mph, travel hundreds of miles per day, and soar as high as 15,000 feet. In Grand Canyon, condors are often spotted soon after sunrise or just before sunset. Although easily confused with turkey vultures, condors have much larger wingspans and triangular white coloring on the underside of their wings. Adult condors are characterized by a pink-orange head and a white underwing coloration. Young condors are almost entirely black. Mature condors, which weigh up to 23 pounds, can live for 50 years or more.

California condors are scavengers that feed exclusively on carrion (the decaying flesh of dead animals). Their powerful bills can break bones and tear out flesh, and their bald heads allow the birds to dig deep into bloody carcasses without dirtying their feathers. Condors typically feed on elk, mule deer and cattle, but they will eat just about anything they can find. Because the supply of carrion is unpredictable, condors eat as much as they can and store excess meat in their "crop," an extension of the esophagus used to store food. Visible on the condor's front chest, the fleshy red crop can hold more than three pounds of meat.

The California condor's range once extended from Canada to Mexico. During the Ice Age, they feasted on the carcasses

California Condor Range

of large animals such as mastodons and giant sloths that roamed North America. But when this "megafauna" went extinct roughly 10,000 years ago, the condor's food supply was severely reduced and the population began to decline. By the time European explorers arrived, condors were found only in western North America. When settlers arrived in the West, condor populations plummeted due to hunting, egg collecting, the ingestion of poisonous bait (left for coyotes), and the ingestion of poisonous lead shot from the carcasses of hunted animals. The condors' slow reproductive rate—they generally lay one egg every two years—exacerbated the problem, and by the 1940s they were only found in southern California.

By 1982 the worldwide California condor population had dropped to just 22 birds. In desperation, the L.A. Zoo and San Diego Zoo began a captive breeding program. In 1987 biologists captured the last wild birds to ensure their safety. A year later, the first captive bred California condor hatched. The condor chick was fed using a condor mother hand puppet, which prevented it from growing accustomed to humans. This was critical if the young condor was to someday fend for itself in the wild.

In 1992 the first captive-raised condors were reintroduced to central California. Four years later, condors were reintroduced to the Vermillion Cliffs in northern Arizona, and those condors soon flew south to the vast spaces of Grand Canyon. It was the first time condors had been seen in Grand Canyon in over 70 years. The Canyon's remote location, rugged terrain, and strong updrafts are perfect for condors, and over the next decade the number of captive bred condors in Grand Canyon grew. In 2003 a wild-bred condor chick successfully fledged (left the nest) in Grand Canyon—the first time a wild condor had fledged anywhere since 1982. As of this writing, seven wild-bred California condors were flying free in Arizona and Utah.

Today there are over 430 California condors, over half of which live in the wild. Arizona and Utah are home to over 70 condors. Although lead poisoning from spent bullets remains the biggest threat to wild condors, groups like The Peregrine Fund (www.peregrinefund.org) are working to ensure a bright future for these magnificent birds.

Peregrine Falcon *(Falco peregrinus)*

Peregrine falcons are birds of prey that can spot victims from thousands of feet above. Once a peregrine selects a target, it dive bombs it at speeds topping 200 mph—the fastest speed of any animal. The collision creates an explosion of feathers, and victims that don't die upon impact have their necks broken by the peregrine's powerful beak. Peregrines are such successful strikers that they were used to kill Nazi carrier pigeons in World War II. By the early 1970s, however, peregrine populations in the U.S. had declined due to hunting and the toxic effects of pesticides. To increase populations, young peregrines were raised in captivity and released in the wild. Today it is estimated that at least 100 pairs of peregrines nest on Grand Canyon's cliffs.

Bald Eagle *(Haliaeetus leucocephalus)*

Famous for their striking white heads, bald eagles are large birds of prey with seven-foot wingspans. Their nests can measure up to 10 feet across and weigh up to 2,000 pounds. Although designated America's national symbol in 1782, by the 1960s there were fewer than 400 nesting pairs of bald eagles in the lower 48 states. Hunting, habitat loss and the effects of pesticides had decimated eagle populations. Today, after decades of conservation efforts, bald eagles have made a remarkable comeback, with over 20,000 nesting pairs in the lower 48 states.

Canyon Wren *(Catherpes mexicanus)*

This small brown and white songbird is famous for its beautiful call, a series of delicate high-pitched whistles that descend in speed and tone. Spend a week floating down the Colorado River and you'll soon learn to recognize the canyon wren's delightful song as it echoes through the Canyon. Canyon wrens are found in the arid mountains and canyonlands of the West, and their range stretches from British Columbia to southern Mexico. Their long, narrow bill is specially designed to pluck insects and spiders from small openings and rock crevices.

Turkey Vulture
(Cathartes aura)

Turkey vultures are often mistaken for California condors in Grand Canyon, but their underwing coloration, which is dominated by white feathers at the outer edges, is the exact opposite of a condor's. Turkey vultures also have a smaller wingspan, which measures "just" six feet across. That said, condors and turkey vultures share many similarities. Both are scavengers that feed on carrion (dead animals), and their bald, featherless head is easy to clean after it's been extracted from the bloody innards of a carcass. Unlike California condors, turkey vultures range from Canada to Argentina, and their worldwide population is estimated at roughly 4.5 million birds. Adult turkey vultures weigh up to five pounds and live up to 16 years in the wild.

Raven (Corvus corax)

Ravens are opportunistic omnivores that eat insects, nuts, small animals, dead animals and garbage. Highly adaptable, they are found from the river to the rim in Grand Canyon, making them one of the park's most commonly spotted birds. Although often mistaken for crows, ravens are significantly larger. They weigh up to 3.5 pounds with a 50-inch wingspan. Ravens have one of the largest brains of any bird, and they can make over 30 calling noises, including their famous "kraaak-krah." Highly acrobatic, they can fly upside down and perform flips and rolls in flight.

Mexican Spotted Owl (Strix occidentalis lucida)

This beautiful owl, one of three subspecies of spotted owl in North America, is officially listed as an endangered species. Among the largest owls in North America, Mexican spotted owls grow up to 19 inches long with a 45-inch wingspan. Adults can weigh up to one and a half pounds. Their range stretches from the Four Corners region to western Texas and down to central Mexico. In northern Arizona they often nest in caves or on cliff edges in rocky canyons. The Mexican spotted owl hunts small mammals at night, and its large eyes provide superior vision in low light. Unlike most owls, the Mexican spotted owl has dark eyes.

Bighorn Sheep

Ovis canadensis

Bighorn sheep are among the most impressive animals in Grand Canyon. Despite weighing up to 220 pounds, bighorns are extremely nimble, hopping along narrow ledges and jumping down 20-foot inclines with grace. Their unique concave hooves, which include a hard outer edge and a soft interior sole, help bighorns grip rocks and navigate steep terrain. Sharp eyesight and keen hearing help them detect predators such as mountain lions, coyotes and bobcats.

Both males (rams) and females (ewes) develop horns shortly after birth. The horns grow larger each year, and annual growth rings indicate a bighorn's age. The ewe's horns never grow past half curl, but the ram's legendary horns curve up and over the ears in a dramatic C-shaped curl. Ram horns can weigh up to 30 pounds and measure three feet in total length. If the horns ever start to block peripheral vision, they are deliberately *broomed* (rubbed down) on rocks. During mating season in the fall, competing rams charge each other head on at speeds topping 20 miles per hour. When rams collide, their horns smash together and produce a loud cracking sound, similar to a rifle shot, which can sometimes be heard for miles. Thickened skulls allow rams to withstand repeated collisions. Rams can fight for over 24 hours, and rams with the biggest horns generally do the most mating. Although rams are independent by nature, they range between herds of ewes during mating season.

Desert bighorn sheep (*Ovis canadensis nelsoni*), which are found in the deserts of the U.S. and Mexico, are a subspecies of bighorn sheep found in much of the West. Well adapted to arid environments, desert bighorns can survive for weeks without water. Grasses constitute the majority of their diet, but they also eat sedges and cacti. Adults can live up to 20 years in the wild. From 1850 to 1950, desert bighorn populations plummeted due to hunting and diseases from domestic sheep. Since 1960, however, desert bighorn numbers have increased substantially thanks to successful conservation measures.

Historic
Bighorn Range

Historic Desert
Bighorn Range

Mountain Lion

Felis concolor

Mountain lions (also known as pumas, cougars or catamounts) range from Canada to Argentina—the most extensive range of any mammal in the Western Hemisphere. Historically they inhabited all 48 lower states, but in the late 1800s and early 1900s mountain lions in the United States were hunted to the brink of extinction (see page 42). Following the enactment of strict hunting regulations, they have made a steady comeback in the West.

Mountain lions are the largest wildcats in North America. Large males weigh up to 250 pounds, and females weigh up to 140 pounds. They are quick, efficient killers that can reach top speeds of 50 mph and travel up to 25 miles a day in search of prey. (One mountain lion in Grand Canyon descended the South Rim, swam across the Colorado River, and climbed to the North Rim in a span of eight hours.) Mountain lions often stalk animals prior to attacking. When they pounce, they can leap over 30 *feet* in a single bound. Victims are often killed with a lethal bite that severs the spinal cord. In Grand Canyon mountain lions feed primarily on mule deer, killing up to one per week, but they also prey on elk, coyote and bighorn sheep. Like all cats, mountain lions require meat to survive, and they will eat just about anything they can catch, including lizards, small rodents and birds. Retractable claws aid in both hunting and tree climbing.

Solitary and territorial, mountain lions require an extensive "home range." In Grand Canyon, the home range can measure up to 185 square miles. Adult mountain lions come together only for mating, and females are exclusively responsible for parenting. Cubs stay with their mother for roughly two years while she protects them and teaches hunting skills. Although born with a spotted coloration, mountain lions develop a uniform tan coloration by about 2.5 years in age.

Reclusive by nature, mountain lions go to great lengths to avoid people, and attacks on humans are extremely rare. If you do encounter a mountain lion in Grand Canyon, however, use extra caution.

Elk

Cervus elaphus

Elk are the largest member of the deer family on the Colorado Plateau and the second-largest member of the deer family in North America after moose. The name "elk" was derived from a European word for moose because early explorers thought elk resembled moose. Male elk (bulls) grow up to eight feet long and weigh up to 800 pounds. Female elk (cows) grow up to seven feet long and weigh up to 500 pounds.

Elk are distinguished from mule deer by their massive size and unique coloration: a tan body with a dark brown "pelage" (coat) above the neck. Shawnee Indians call elk *wapiti*, "White Rump," due to their white backside. In the fall, however, massive antlers are an elk's most distinguishing characteristic. Antlers, which grow only on bulls, can reach four feet in length and weigh up to 40 pounds. They are shed each spring, and over the next three to four months new antlers grow back at the rate of about one half inch per day, reaching maximum size in time for the rut (mating season). During the rut, which generally lasts from late summer to mid-November, bulls emit a bugle-like sound as a sign of dominance and a challenge to other bulls. The bugle starts off as a bellow and changes to a shrill scream that can often be heard for miles. Dominance between bulls is determined in contests where bulls engage in antler wrestling. The most dominant bulls assemble a harem of a dozen or more cows, and the cows give birth in the spring

Elk are ruminants with four-chambered stomachs, and they forage on grasses, plants, leaves and bark. On average, they eat about 20 pounds of vegetation a day. In Grand Canyon elk are often seen grazing near Grand Canyon Village. Although they have become accustomed to humans and appear docile, elk should never be approached, especially during the rut.

In the early 1900s, elk were eliminated from the Southwest due to overhunting. The elk you see in Grand Canyon today are actually descendents of elk transplanted from Yellowstone National Park between 1913 and 1928.

Mule Deer

Odocoileus hemionus

Mule deer are one of the most commonly spotted large mammal in the park. They are named for their large ears that move independently of each other, much like a mule's. Although closely related to white-tailed deer, mule deer are slightly larger, have larger ears, and have white tails with a black tip.

Mule deer are found in the western U.S., and their range extends from western Canada to central Mexico. In the Southwest U.S., mule deer are found predominantly in mountainous areas. Like elk, they are ruminants with multi-chambered stomachs. In the summer they forage on plants, leaves and brushy vegetation. In the winter they forage on conifers such as juniper and ponderosa pine. Mule deer are much smaller than elk, however, with bucks (males) weighing 150 to 300 pounds and does (females) weighing 95 to 200 pounds. Adult mule deer often measure five to seven feet in length.

Bucks grow a large pair of antlers each year, then shed them each winter. The annual cycle of antler growth is regulated by changes in the length of the day. During the fall rut (mating season), bucks compete for the right to breed with females. Although conflict between bucks is infrequent, mild fights sometimes break out. In such cases bucks enmesh their antlers while trying to force the head of the other buck down. Although serious injuries are rare, antlers sometimes become locked together. If the deer are unable to unlock antlers, they will be unable to eat, and they will ultimately die of starvation. Conflict between does is far more common, so family groups tend to be spaced widely apart.

Breeding occurs in the fall, and gestation lasts 190 to 200 days. Young does give birth to one fawn, but older does often give birth to twins. Fawns are able to distinguish their mother through a unique odor produced by glands on the mother's hind legs. Fawns are born with white spots on their backs, which help camouflage them with the dappled light of the forest floor. As fawns grow older, their spots disappear. Adult mule deer can live 9–11 years in the wild. Common predators in Grand Canyon include mountain lions, bobcats and coyotes.

Bobcat

Lynx rufus

Ranging from the deserts of the Southwest to the swamps of Florida, bobcats are North America's most common wildcat. But they are highly elusive animals that are rarely seen or heard. Bobcats typically spend the day resting, then wander for miles around dusk and dawn in search of prey. Their diet includes a wide range of small animals such as rabbits, squirrels, birds and snakes. Bobcats rarely chase their prey, however, preferring to seek out a hiding spot and lie in wait. When a victim approaches, the bobcat pounces, snagging its prey with sharp, retractable claws. The name "bobcat" comes from the cat's stubby "bobbed" tail. With an average weight of 20 pounds, bobcats are larger than house cats, but they share many of the same personality traits, including hissing, purring and using trees as scratching posts. Like most felines, bobcats are largely solitary, and males and females come together only for mating. Females generally have litters of two or three kittens, and those that reach adulthood typically live six to eight years in the wild.

Coyote

canis latrans

Historically confined to the open spaces of the West, coyotes spread rapidly throughout the U.S. following the extermination of wolves in the 1800s. Today coyotes are found in all lower 48 states. Intelligent and adaptable, they are found in all of Grand Canyon's ecological zones, from the deserts at the bottom of the Canyon to the spruce-fir forests high on the North Rim. Coyotes typically hunt in pairs, and they can reach top speeds of 43 mph. Their diet consists mostly of small mammals, but coyotes are omnivores that will eat just about anything, including birds, snakes, insects and trash. They can weigh up to 30 pounds, and their brownish-red coat turns grey in the winter. In native legends Coyote is often portrayed as a scheming, meddling trickster who scrapes by on cunning and charm. The word "coyote" is derived from the Aztec word *cóyotl*, meaning "trickster." Coyote's Latin name, *Canis latrans*, means "barking dog."

Grand Canyon Rattlesnake

Crotalus viridis abyssus

There are six species of rattlesnakes in Grand Canyon, but the Grand Canyon Rattlesnake is the most famous by far. A subspecies of the Western Rattlesnake, it evolved over millions of years in the depths of Grand Canyon. Today Grand Canyon is the only place in the world where the Grand Canyon Rattlesnake is found. It is distinguished by its pale, pinkish coloration and irregular dark blotches that become pale toward the center. Like all rattlesnakes, the Grand Canyon Rattlesnake has poor eyesight but a sharp sense of smell. It can also detect body heat through infrared sensors located on either side of its head. These keen senses are used to detect prey while a rattler lies in wait. When the snake strikes, it injects a paralyzing venom through sharp fangs. Once the victim is motionless, the rattler swallows it whole. Rattlesnakes, in turn, are preyed upon by eagles and hawks, which pluck rattlers from the ground and drop them repeatedly from the air to kill them.

Kaibab Squirrel

Sciurus aberti kaibabensis

This beautiful squirrel is found only in the ponderosa pine forests of the Kaibab Plateau, an area measuring roughly 20 miles by 40 miles alongside Grand Canyon's North Rim. In behavior and biology, the Kaibab squirrel is nearly identical to the Abert's squirrel, which is common on Grand Canyon's South Rim. But whereas the Abert's squirrel has a white belly and a gray tail, the Kaibab squirrel has a dark belly and a white tail. Scientists believe that long ago both squirrels belonged to the same species. As global temperatures fluctuated during the Ice Age, however, an isolated population of squirrels was confined to the Kaibab plateau, and it gradually evolved into its own distinct subspecies. Both the Kaibab squirrel and the Abert's squirrel depend on ponderosa pines as a major food source, eating both the tender bark and the seeds from pine cones.

HISTORY

HUMANS FIRST SET eyes on Grand Canyon roughly 10,000 years ago, when primitive hunters and gatherers first arrived in Arizona. Little is known about these prehistoric people, but small artifacts found in the backs of caves confirm their existence in Grand Canyon. Among the objects discovered were spear points and small split-twig figurines twisted into the shapes of animals. Some of the animal figurines were pierced with tiny spears made of agave thorns, indicating that hunting played an important role in their lives.

What ultimately happened to these early settlers is unclear. It's possible that they abandoned Grand Canyon, but it's just as likely that they stayed. In either case, a new culture called the Ancestral Puebloans (aka Anasazi) appeared several thousand years later. The Ancestral Puebloans occupied the Four Corners region from roughly A.D. 0 to 1200, and for over a thousand years they flourished in Grand Canyon, which marked the westernmost range of their territory.

Archaeologists have subdivided the Ancestral Puebloans into two distinct cultural groups: the Basketmakers and the Pueblo Anasazi. The Basketmakers lived from A.D. 0 to 700. Named for their exceptional skill at basketry, they wove plant fibers into beautiful baskets and sandals. Because they were hunter-gatherers, the Basketmakers were constantly on the move in search of food, but as time passed they discovered agriculture, which allowed them to settle down in one place. They constructed dwellings in caves or under overhanging cliffs, and they grew beans, corn and squash nearby.

Although farming was the Basketmakers' main source of food, they also hunted animals with spears, which provided them with food and raw materials for clothing. In the winter, Basketmakers wore robes made of deer skin, rabbit skin, or turkey feathers. In the summer they wore loin clothes and skirts woven from plant fibers. Jewelry was made from seashells imported along trade routes from the Pacific Coast, and live parrots were imported from Mexico. The Basketmakers kept dogs as pets, smoked tobacco from pipes, and played music on six-hole flutes. By A.D. 600 they had also learned to make pottery.

Around A.D. 700 the Basketmakers discovered the bow and arrow, which allowed them to hunt more food in less time. With more free time on their hands they continued to advance technologically, and soon they were using stone masonry to build impressive stone villages under the awnings of cliffs. Some of these dwellings, such as Canyon de Chelly in northeast Arizona and Chaco Canyon in New Mexico, are among of the most spectacular archaeological ruins in the United States.

As Ancestral Puebloan lifestyles advanced, so did the rules governing their society. Customs and social codes became highly developed, with some villages operating like independent city-states. Archaeologists consider these later Ancestral Puebloans part of the second cultural group: the Pueblo Anasazi.

The Pueblo Anasazi built irrigation ditches near fertile areas and stored surplus crops in granaries (stone storage compartments). Artistic achievements also blossomed during this time. Cotton was spun and woven into beautiful clothes, dwellings were covered with murals and pictographs, and elaborate costumes were used in religious ceremonies. By A.D. 1100 the Ancestral Puebloans were flourishing, occupying thousands of sites in and around Grand Canyon. Their technological achievements were extraordinary, placing them among the most advanced Indians north of Mexico. Then, at the height of their prosperity, the Ancestral Puebloans mysteriously abandoned their settlements and vanished from Grand Canyon.

Archaeologists are at a loss to explain the swift departure of the Ancestral Puebloans. Some believe they fell victim to a massive drought. Others blame a depletion of natural resources. Still others think there was a great war between neighboring tribes. Unfortunately, little evidence remains to provide a clear picture of what actually happened. Whatever the cause, after abandoning Grand Canyon many Ancestral Puebloans moved south and merged with the Hopi and Zuni tribes. Within a few centuries, other tribes including the Havasupai, Hualapai, Southern Paiute, and Navajo had settled the surrounding territory.

Ancestral Puebloan Pottery

Mystery of the Ancestral Puebloans

THE SWIFT DECLINE of the Ancestral Puebloans is one of the Southwest's greatest archaeological mysteries. Why would a culture at the height of its prosperity—by many accounts the most advanced culture north of Mexico—suddenly abandon its settlements? What caused them to flee the Four Corners region they had occupied for over 1,000 years, never to return?

For decades archaeologists believed that the Ancestral Puebloans fell victim to a massive drought. The entire Southwest experienced a period of decreased rainfall in the late 1200s, and it seemed logical to connect this drought to the ancient culture's demise. But recent evidence suggests the so-called Great Drought may not have been enough to cause a complete cultural collapse. The Ancestral Puebloans, it turns out, started to abandon their settlements prior to the drought. And they had survived worse droughts in the past. Why should another drought be different?

Some archaeologists believe the abandonment was triggered by a depletion of the region's scarce natural resources, which could have led to social and political upheaval—possibly even war. In fact, many Ancestral Puebloan structures built near the end appear to be defensive in nature. But if there was a war, why didn't the winners stay to enjoy the spoils?

Some archaeologists believe the demise of the Ancestral Puebloans was triggered by a religious collapse. Religion and daily life were one and the same to the Ancestral Puebloans, and a collapse of one could have led to a collapse of the other. Faced with failing crops, chronic shortages, and rain dances that no longer worked, the Ancestral Puebloans may have lost faith in their prevailing religion. At the same time, the Hopi's new Katsina religion was gaining momentum to the south. With its colored masks and lurid dances, the Katsina movement may have lured the Ancestral Puebloans away from their homeland. A few archaeologists have speculated that some Ancestral Puebloans may have moved as far away as Mexico.

While each of these theories offers a possible explanations, many unanswered questions remain. Until new evidence comes to light, the full story of the Ancestral Puebloans will remain one of Grand Canyon's best-kept secrets.

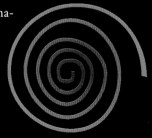

CANYON TRIBES

HOPI

The Hopi are one of the oldest tribes in the region, having lived in northeast Arizona for over 1,000 years. Oraibi, a Hopi village 80 miles east of Grand Canyon, was settled over 800 years ago, making it the oldest continuously inhabited town in the United States. Grand Canyon is a deeply symbolic place for the Hopi, who believe that both people and animals emerged from the Grand Canyon at a place called the *Sipapuni*, a mineral spring located near the junction of the Colorado and Little Colorado Rivers. Upon dying, the Hopi believe that their spirits will pass back through the Sipapuni. Hopi religion revolves around *Katsinas*, spirit beings who visit Hopi villages for a few months each year, performing good deeds, punishing criminals, and bringing rain. Most Katsinas are believed to live on Humphrey's Peak, the tallest of the San Francisco Peaks just north of Flagstaff. The Hopi craft hundreds of brightly painted wooden dolls, called *Tihu*, to represent different Katsinas. Tihu—also called Kachina Dolls—are traditionally carved from a single piece of cottonwood root and given to children to teach them about the different Katsinas.

Hopi Tihu

SOUTHERN PAIUTE

The Southern Paiute settled the plateau country north of Grand Canyon around A.D. 1300. Because of the region's limited resources, they found it easier to exist in small bands rather than as large groups governed by complex social structures. Each band had an individual leader who acted as a tribal advisor. The leader was generally an elderly man who had spent a lifetime studying the landscape, and he imparted his knowledge of plants and animals to the tribe. The Southern Paiute hunted deer and small game on the Kaibab Plateau, which encompasses much of Grand Canyon's North Rim. *Kaibab* is derived from a Paiute word meaning "Mountain Lying Down." While the men hunted, the women gathered plants. Over time, the Southern Paiute also adopted agriculture from the nearby Hopi and Navajo tribes.

HAVASUPAI

The Havasupai have been living in western Grand Canyon for over 700 years. The name *Havasupai*, "People of the Blue-Green Water," is a reference to the beautiful turquoise pools and waterfalls found in Havasu Canyon (p.283). Because the Havasupai had access to constant water, they grew more food than any other tribe in the region. Havasu Creek, one of the most dependable water sources in Grand Canyon, helped the Havasupai weather even the greatest droughts. In the winter, when the narrow walls of Havasu Canyon only let in a few hours of sunlight each day, the Havasupai traveled to the vast forests along the South Rim to gather plants and hunt game.

The *Hualapai*, "Pine Tree People," are close neighbors of the Havasupai. Although listed as two separate tribes by early American explorers, the Havasupai and Hualapai consider themselves members of the same *Pai* culture. The Hualapai spent most of their time in the forested plateaus above Grand Canyon, but in the summer they would sometimes gather plants in the rugged side canyons along the South Rim.

NAVAJO

The Navajo were one of the last tribes to settle the region, arriving from northwest Canada 500 to 1,000 years ago. Upon reaching the desert, they were forced to adopt a new way of life. Unable to survive on their own, they raided the villages of previously settled tribes, but eventually they learned agriculture from their new neighbors. Traditional Navajo homes are called *hogans*, one-room buildings built out of logs and tree branches that always face east so the Navajo can start each day by greeting the light of the rising sun. The Navajo believe humans must live in harmony with nature, achieving a sense of place called *hozho*. They refer to themselves *Dine*, "The People." In the 1600s Spaniards introduced sheep to the Navajo, and before long Navajo culture revolved around sheep herding. Sheep meat replaced deer meat as the primary source of protein in the Navajo diet, and sheep wool was woven into beautiful rugs with colorful designs. Navajo legend speaks of two animal beings, Spider Man and Spider Woman, who taught the Navajo how to build looms and weave.

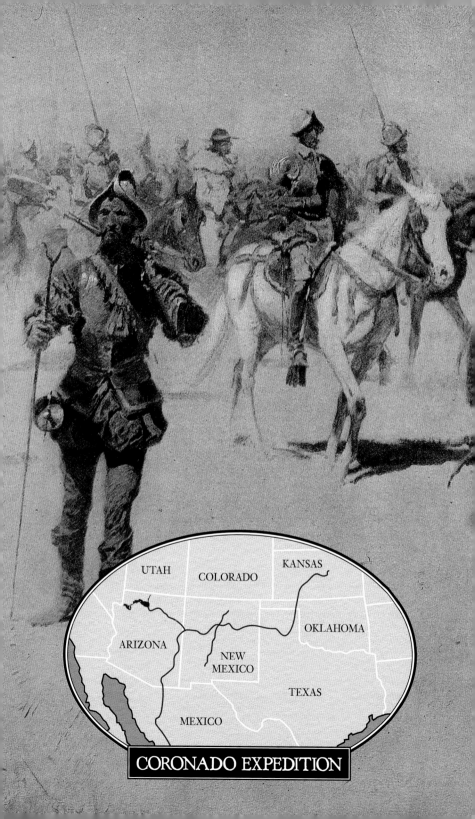

CORONADO EXPEDITION

A FABLED CITY OF GOLD

LESS THAN 30 years after Columbus discovered North America, Spanish conquistador Hernán Cortéz defeated the Aztecs in Mexico. At the time, Spain was the most powerful country in the world, and its sprawling empire covered much of Europe and the New World. But maintaining these far-flung properties was an expensive proposition, and despite the vast wealth plundered from the Aztecs, Spain was soon desperate for additional funds.

In 1529 a Spanish vessel shipwrecked off the Texas coast. The wreck's four survivors spent the next seven years wandering the desert, and when they finally returned to Mexico they told stories of a fabulous city of gold located somewhere in the American Southwest. This city, referred to as the Seven Cities of Cibola, quickly captured the imagination of Spain.

In 1540 Spanish authorities organized a military expedition to locate the Seven Cities of Cibola. Led by charismatic, 29-year-old Francisco Vásquez de Coronado, the expedition consisted of 300 Spanish men, several hundred Indians, and thousands of cattle, sheep and goats. Five months later, the expedition reached the spot where the Seven Cities were rumored to be located, but all that they found was a small Indian village.

Coronado was dejected, but the Indians told him of a larger group of seven cities to the west. Coronado immediately dispatched his lieutenant, Don Pedro de Tovar, to investigate these claims. When Tovar returned, he reported that he had failed to locate the Seven Cites of Cibola, but he had learned of a mighty river to the west. Hoping this river was the gateway to Cibola, Coronado dispatched another search party under the command of García López de Cárdenas.

After three weeks of harrowing travel, Cárdenas' party became the first Europeans to set eyes on Grand Canyon. But they were hardly impressed by what they saw. From their vantage point on the South Rim—believed to be somewhere between Moran Point and Desert View—the Spaniards estimated that the Colorado River was just six feet wide. (In fact, the average width of the Colorado in Grand Canyon is closer to 300 feet.) Although their Hopi guides insisted that the river was much larger, the Spaniards refused to believe them. They had never encountered a natural landmark of such a vast scale, and they were unable to comprehend its true dimensions.

For three days the Spaniards tried to find a route to the river. One group of soldiers made it one-third of the way down, but they were unable to descend any farther. Even at that depth, they were shocked to discover rocks that had appeared only a few feet high were taller than the 185-foot tower of Seville in Spain. Suddenly comprehending Grand Canyon's true dimensions, Cárdenas turned his men around. Coronado's expedition ultimately traveled as far as present-day Kansas, but the Seven Cities of Cibola were never found.

THE SECOND SPANISH WAVE

IN THE DECADES following Coronado's expedition, Spain once again ignored the American Southwest. No colonization attempts were made until 1598, when Juan de Onate founded Santa Fe, New Mexico. Within a few decades, Spanish missions had spread west towards Hopi towns.

The Hopi resented the proselytizing missionaries. They had no interest in changing their religious beliefs, and they did not want the Spaniards interfering in their daily lives. Before long, Indian mistrust reached a breaking point. In 1680 leaders from several tribes met in secret to plan a coordinated revolt against the Spanish. The Pueblo Revolt, as it was later called, drove out the Spanish and allowed the Indians to regain control of their territories. But their victory was short-lived. Twelve years later, a more powerful Spanish army marched north to reconquer the Southwest. As the army approached, the Hopi retreated to the tops of tall mesas, which were easily defended from above. Hopi mesas soon became a favored refuge for Indians fleeing the Spanish throughout the Southwest.

While battles raged to the east of Grand Canyon, Indians living in the remote western Grand Canyon remained relatively undisturbed. Then, in 1776, a Franciscan missionary named Francisco Tomás Garcés attempted to blaze a trail between the Spanish missions in California and the missions along the Rio Grande. His journey led him up the Colorado River into western Grand Canyon, where he encountered the Havasupai Indians. The Havasupai graciously invited Garcés to stay for five days of feasting—an offer that he gladly accepted. When the feast was over, Garcés set out to visit the Hopi villages to the east. But the Hopi, stung by years of warfare, were deeply suspicious of the Spaniard. They refused to feed Garcés or even accept his gifts. Taking the hint, Garcés returned to Havasu Canyon, where he was greeted with another multi-day feast.

Not long after Garcés' journey, another Spanish expedition, the Dominguez-Escalante party, left New Mexico to find a northern route to the Pacific. By the time they reached the Sierra Nevada Mountains, however, deep snows had already set in and the mountains were impassable. Forced to abandon their mission, the Spaniards headed south, at one point crossing the Colorado River near the northern tip of Grand Canyon. The Dominguez-Escalante party thus became the third and final Spanish expedition to set eyes on Grand Canyon.

Although the Spanish had relatively little contact with Indians living near Grand Canyon, their indirect presence had a huge impact on Indian life. The Spanish introduced horses, cattle and sheep to North America—animals that would come to define many Southwestern tribes. New fruits such as peaches, melons and figs were also introduced. But along with these positive influences came deadly diseases such as smallpox, which had a devastating impact on Indian populations throughout the Southwest.

AMERICAN EXPLORERS

IN 1821 MEXICO gained independence from Spain and acquired much of the American Southwest. But Mexico, like Spain, generally avoided the desolate region, and Indians living near Grand Canyon remained relatively undisturbed. But a new power was looming on the eastern horizon.

Following the Louisiana Purchase in 1803, American beaver trappers began fanning out across the West. Soon they were scouring the wild streams that tumbled down from the Rockies into the Four Corners region. But even then Grand Canyon was generally avoided as a destination. Although beavers lived at the bottom of the Canyon, reaching them proved too arduous a task.

Not that some trappers didn't try. In 1826 a trapping party led by Ewing Young traveled up the Colorado River on foot. They became the first Americans to set eyes on Grand Canyon, but their journey was a miserable one. At one point the men plodded through 18 inches of snow and ate bark to fend off starvation. Not surprisingly, they found little to like about the region. As one of the trappers remembered, "We arrived where the river emerges from these horrid mountains, which so cage it up, as to deprive all human beings of the ability to descend to its banks, and make use of its waters."

Such descriptions did little to encourage further exploration. With its extreme climate, physically challenging terrain, and striking lack of water, the Four Corners region was a terrible place to settle—which was precisely why Mormon leader Brigham Young decided to settle there.

THE ILL-FATED EXPLORER

IN 1857 THE U.S. War Department sent novice Lieutenant Joseph Ives on an expedition to explore the lower reaches of the Colorado River. Unfortunately for Ives, the expedition's 50-foot steamboat, *The Explorer*, was poorly designed to handle the rapids, shallows, and sand bars of the Colorado. The boat ran aground countless times, and the crew was often forced to unload and tow the boat by hand. After two months of slow progress and much towing, *The Explorer* struck a boulder near the present site of Hoover Dam. The crew was tossed overboard and the boat was wrecked beyond repair.

Defeated, Ives declared that he had reached the farthest point of navigation on the river. Not only was his statement untrue, Ives had already been proven wrong. Several weeks earlier, a man named George Johnson, incensed at being passed over by the War Department to lead the historic journey, had steamed his own boat past the point where *The Explorer* wrecked.

Ives's expedition produced several fine maps of the region, but much of the Colorado River remained a mystery. Writing in his log, Ives concluded his journey with the unfortunate remark: "The region is, of course, altogether valueless. It can be approached only from the south, and after entering it there is nothing to do but leave. Ours has been the first, and will doubtless be the last, party of whites to visit this profitless locality."

Today Grand Canyon, Hoover Dam, and nearby Las Vegas attract over 40 million visitors each year.

Fleeing religious persecution in Illinois, Young led his followers to Utah's Great Salt Lake in 1846. The desolate landscape offered the perfect refuge for the Mormons—a place where they could practice their new religion in peace. Over the next two decades, Mormon settlements spread south, representing the first significant white presence anywhere near Grand Canyon. But even the notoriously rugged Mormons refused to explore Grand Canyon's depths. That job would fall to a 34-year-old geology professor named John Wesley Powell.

JOHN WESLEY POWELL

IN 1848, FOLLOWING the conclusion of the Mexican War, the United States acquired the vast chunk of land that would one day make up California, Nevada, Arizona, Utah, Colorado, and New Mexico. But even by the 1860s, maps of the United States had a single word splashed across the Grand Canyon region: UNEXPLORED. Most men, even the heroically rugged trappers who had opened up much of the West, took one look at those maps and stayed away. But one man looked at the maps and saw an opportunity for everlasting fame.

John Wesley Powell was probably the least likely man in America to conquer the Colorado River. A one-armed college professor with virtually no whitewater experience, he was a case study in everything that *wasn't* needed to successfully navigate the river. At five feet six inches tall, he hardly cut an imposing figure. But what Powell lacked in physical stature he more than made up for in personal ambition.

In 1868 Powell decided to organize an expedition to explore the Colorado River and the desolate canyon country it flowed through. He went to Washington, D.C. to raise money for the trip, but with the federal treasury still reeling from the Civil War, government funds were hard to come by. Powell was offered some

HERO or LIAR?

JAMES WHITE

In 1867, two years before Powell's expedition, a raft was pulled from the Colorado River just below Grand Canyon. On board was a starving, sunburned, half-naked man named James White, who proceeded to tell a story so amazing that it is still disputed to this day. White claimed to have spent the previous two weeks floating down the Colorado lashed to a raft, making him the first man to successfully run Grand Canyon. Most modern scholars dispute White's story, based mostly on the fact that it's so hard to believe. But supposing it's true, White's journey would have been one of the most remarkable whitewater adventures of all time.

military rations, however, which he gladly accepted. Undaunted, he ultimately managed to scrape together funding from a variety of private institutions.

Powell's next step was to assemble a crew. The job offered no pay, harsh living conditions, and life-threatening risks. Not surprisingly, the men who accepted these terms were reckless, crazy, or a little of both. Most were trappers and mountain men eager for adventure and excitement. But to Powell, the journey was primarily a scientific expedition. "The object," he wrote, "is to make collections in geology, natural history, antiquities, and ethnology."

On May 24, 1869 Powell's expedition launched four boats from Green River City, Wyoming. Their starting point was 6,100 feet above sea level. Their destination—Grand Wash Cliffs, near present-day Lake Mead—lay at an elevation of 1,300 feet. How the river got there was anyone's guess.

For the first week of their journey, the men floated peacefully down the Green River. The one-armed Powell, unable to row, sat perched on a chair tied to his boat. At first the lazy current bored the men, but soon the river started to intensify. As they continued downstream, the rapids became frequent and fierce. Then on June 9, one of the boats slipped into a large rapid before the crew had a chance to scout it. The boat plunged into the whitewater and smashed on a rock, splintering into pieces. The three men onboard managed to swim to safety, but a third of the expedition's supplies were lost.

rescue by
UNDERWEAR!

In desolation Canyon, Powell and a crew member named George Bradley set out to climb the steep cliffs above the river. As the one-armed Powell neared the top he became stranded on the edge of a cliff. "Standing on my toes my muscles began to tremble," he wrote. "If I lose my hold I shall fall to the bottom." Powell called to Bradley, who quickly appeared on a ledge above. With time running out, Bradley stripped off his long johns and lowered them down, but they dangled behind Powell just out of reach. Taking a deep breath, Powell leaned back into space and grabbed for the long johns with his one good hand. Catching a pant leg, Powell held on for dear life while Bradley hauled him up to safety.

Powell Expedition Boats

Following Disaster Falls (as Powell later named it) a nervous energy settled over the crew. They were only two weeks into their journey, and they had already lost one of their boats. What would happen if they lost another? The rapids were growing worse, and soon they would be hundreds of miles from civilization.

Determined, the men carried on. For the next two months they followed the Green River as it passed through Wyoming and Utah, running rapids whenever they could but spending most of their time lining or portaging. Lining involved guiding the boats downstream as the men held on to ropes from the shore. It was excruciating work. The ropes burned the men's hands and they were constantly slipping on wet rocks. The alternative was portaging, which entailed carrying the boats—and several thousand pounds of supplies—on shore past the rapid.

By the time the expedition reached the confluence of the Green River and the Grand River (the official start of the Colorado), supplies were running low. They were down to several pounds of spoiled bacon, a few sacks of flour, and some dried apples. The men tried to supplement their diet by hunting, but game in the region was scarce. Before long, the constant hunger and backbreaking days were taking a serious toll on group morale.

On August 4 the expedition reached the start of Grand Canyon. Drifting through the Canyon's upper reaches, Powell was spellbound by the variety of rocks he saw. He thought the highly polished limestone looked like marble, so he named the initial stretch Marble Canyon. Soon the cliffs rose thousands of feet on either side. The scale of the canyon was breathtaking. "We are three quarters of a mile in the depths of the Earth," Powell wrote, "and the great river shrinks into insignificance, as it dashes its angry waves against the walls and cliffs, that rise to the world above; they are but puny ripples, and we are but pygmies."

While Powell marveled at the natural spectacle, many of the crew felt confined. The Canyon was like a prison to them. Daytime highs topped 100°F and the rapids were frequent and fierce. Before long, many began to openly regret their decision to come.

Continuing on, the men twisted deep in the heart of the Canyon. Soon they were fighting off rapids the size of three-story buildings. Even worse, they had no idea what to expect around each bend in the river. There were rumors of giant waterfalls in Grand Canyon, and if those rumors proved true the expedition would find itself trapped at the bottom of a mile deep chasm. Physically and mentally, the men were starting to unwind. They were now down to starvation rations and the threat of death was real.

On August 27 the men were camped above their worst rapid yet. Many in the group doubted they could run it and survive. That night at dinner, a man named Oramel Howland took Powell aside. Howland told Powell that he and two others were abandoning the expedition. They would take their chances climbing out of the Canyon—a decision that carried equally lethal implications.

Powell respected the men's decision, but he was convinced the rapid could be run. And according to his calculations, the group was no more than 50 miles from the end of their journey. He spent all night trying to convince the men not to leave, but they had seen enough. The three men left the following morning. They were never seen again.

Concentrating on the matter at hand, Powell studied the rapid. The river was hemmed in by steep cliffs, so there was no possibility of portaging. And other than a small section at the top of the rapid, lining was also out of the question. With a slimmed down crew, the men abandoned one of the boats and lined the remaining two boats as far as they could. Then they swooped down into the rapid.

The first boat rushed down a steep wave and was swamped with water. The men pulled for their lives. Soon the waves grew too large to do anything but hold on tight. The boats tossed and turned but somehow managed to stay upright. Before the men knew it, the rapid was behind them. Both boats had survived.

Two days later, Powell's expedition reached the end of its journey. As they approached the confluence of the Colorado and the Virgin Rivers, the men saw several Mormons fishing in the river. The Mormons had been posted there for weeks, under orders from Brigham Young to keep their eyes out "for any fragments or relics of [Powell's] party that might drift down the stream." They were shocked to see Powell and his men alive.

The hearts of the skeletal river runners were filled with joy. The Mormons cooked them a meal, and as one crew member recalled, "we laid our dignified manners aside and assumed the manner of so many hogs. Ate as long as we could and went to sleep to wake up hungry." After 99 days on the river, their voyage was finally over.

Powell's death-defying expedition is virtually impossible to imagine today. River guides who have spent decades rowing the modern, dam-controlled Colorado simply shake their heads in amazement when asked about Powell's historic journey. His under-supplied, ragtag collection of mountain men conquered the wildest, most unpredictable river in North America. Today their journey is often referred to the last great expedition of the American West.

JOHN WESLEY POWELL

JOHN WESLEY POWELL'S Colorado River expedition was one of the greatest adventures in American history. But nearly as remarkable as the expedition is the man who organized it all.

John Wesley Powell was born in 1834, the son of a poor itinerant preacher who moved his family across the frontier. As a young man Powell was constantly on the go, enrolling in several different colleges but never staying around long enough to graduate from any of them. When the Civil War broke out, Powell enlisted on the Union side, making Lieutenant within his first two months. At the battle of Shiloh he was shot in his right arm—an injury that required amputation. Refusing to be kept out of the fight, Powell returned to action several months later and accompanied General Sherman on his conquest of Georgia.

Following the war, Powell underwent an operation to ease the constant pain in his amputated arm. The operation failed, and for the rest of his life Powell was plagued with chronic pain from the raw nerve endings at the end of his stump. Not one to dwell on personal misfortune, Powell simply looked to the future as he tried to figure out what to do with his life. "You are a maimed man," his father told him, "Settle down at teaching. It is a noble profession. Get this nonsense of science and adventure out of your mind."

Powell tried to settle down at teaching, but the lure of the West proved too powerful. As a geologist he had led research trips to the headwaters of the Colorado and Green Rivers—two rivers whose waters ultimately flow through Grand Canyon. It was there that Powell developed an obsession with the Southwest. Powell the geologist was convinced that the canyons of the Colorado would give "the best geological section on the continent." Powell the adventurer desperately wanted to be the first to conquer the final frontier of the United States.

And conquer it he did. Following his Grand Canyon expedition, Powell achieved international fame. On the lecture circuit, he spoke to packed houses and stayed in the finest hotels. Later, he used his influence to help found the Bureau of American Ethnology and the U.S. Geological Survey.

Powell died in 1902. Shortly before his death, he made an unusual bet with his friend W.J. McGee, president of the National Geographic Society. Although physically smaller than McGee, Powell was convinced his brain was larger. To settle the dispute, the men left instructions to have their brains weighed following their deaths. At 1,488 grams, Powell's brain was five percent heavier. Today it rests in a jar at the Smithsonian Institute.

EARLY SETTLERS

JOHN WESLEY POWELL'S journey inaugurated a wave of expeditions to map and explore Grand Canyon. Leading this charge was Powell himself. Shortly after his historic near-death, near-mutiny expedition, Powell announced plans to lead a second trip down the Colorado. Many of his scientific notes had been lost on the first journey, and he was determined to fill in the blanks. This time, however, he would break his trip into stages with supply points along the way, significantly reducing the risks involved. And so in 1871, the indefatigable Powell conquered the Colorado yet again.

Between river trips Powell conducted scientific expeditions along the rim, but these excursions were only temporary, and the region as a whole remained largely uninhabited by whites. Following the arrival of the railroad in northern Arizona in the early 1880s, however, a handful of drifters started taking up permanent residence along the South Rim.

Most of the South Rim's early settlers were miners searching for riches in the depths of Grand Canyon. Although a number of potential mining sites were located, the costs of excavation soon proved prohibitively expensive. Ore had to be packed out on burros, water was scarce, and the closest railroad was two days away. Mining Grand Canyon, it tuned out, was an extremely unprofitable endeavor. But just as that realization started to sink in, the miners discovered another source of revenue: tourists.

Starting in the mid-1880s, people began arriving at Grand Canyon for no other reason than to visit, relax, and take in the views. This was a strikingly new concept. For hundreds of years, Grand Canyon had been avoided—even detested—as a destination. Now, people thought it was beautiful. It was an idea that would turn out to be highly contagious.

The first tourists arrived at the South Rim in 1884 and stayed in makeshift lodges built by miners. Most visitors arrived by stagecoach from the nearby towns of Flagstaff, Williams, and Ash Fork. But the journey was a rugged one. The dirt roads were filled with potholes, and the trip often required at least two days of bone-jarring travel.

It wasn't long before people began looking for a better form of transportation to the South Rim. In 1885 Grand Canyon entrepreneur Bill Bass lured a railroad agent to his lodge to try to convince him of the potential of a spur line to the South Rim. The agent was hardly impressed by what he saw. "No one," he wrote to his superiors, "would go that far only to see a hole in the ground."

It would take over a decade for the railroads to realize their mistake. When they finally did, the previously isolated Grand Canyon would find itself linked directly to the modern world—and visitors would arrive by the thousands.

GRAND CANYON PIONEERS

JOHN HANCE

JOHN HANCE was the first permanent white settler in Grand Canyon. After visiting on a prospecting trip in 1881, he fell in love with the scenery. Two years later, he built a log cabin east of Grandview Point and started renting out rooms to guests.

Hance is fondly remembered as Grand Canyon's premier storyteller, but his stories rarely contained a shred of truth. He took great pleasure in spinning tall tales with a deadpan delivery until his hapless listeners realized they'd been had. When Hance was once asked how the Canyon formed, he responded, "It was hard work, took a long time, but I dug it myself, with a pick and a shovel. If you want to know what I done with the dirt, just look south through a clearin' in the trees at what they call the San Francisco Peaks." Hance had hundreds of stories in his repertoire, and he never told the same story twice in exactly the same way.

As Hance once confided to a friend, "I've got to tell stories to them people for their money; and if I don't tell it to them, who will? I can make these tenderfeet believe that a frog eats boiled eggs; and I'm going to do it; and I'm going to make 'em believe that he carries it a mile to find a rock to crack it on."

The tenderfeet loved it. According to one early visitor, "Anyone who comes to the Grand Canyon and fails to meet John Hance will miss half the show." In 1906 he was offered free room and board at the Bright Angel Lodge in exchange for just hanging out with the guests and being himself.

JOHN D. LEE

BEFORE HE WAS banished to the Grand Canyon by Brigham Young, John D. Lee had been a prosperous Mormon living in southern Utah with his 19 wives. But in 1857 Lee participated in the Mountain Meadow Massacre, in which a group of Mormons slaughtered a wagon train of 120 pioneers on their way to California. In a blatant cover up, the Mormon Church placed the blame solely on Lee's shoulders. With the law at his back, Lee fled to Grand Canyon.

Lee arrived at a spot along the Colorado River just south of present-day Lake Powell and established Lees Ferry. It was the only viable river crossing for hundreds of miles. But being a wanted man and owning the only ferry crossing for hundreds of miles turned out to be a dangerous combination. In 1874 the law finally caught up with Lee, and he was tried and executed. He was survived by his 53 children.

BILL BASS

BILL BASS moved to Williams, Arizona from New Jersey in 1883. Several years later, curiosity and prospecting brought him to the South Rim, where he spent the next 41 years of his life.

Bass came to Grand Canyon to prospect, but he soon turned to tourism as his main source of income. He built a crude tent camp along the South Rim, and he promoted the camp through home-made lantern slides that were displayed throughout the country.

In 1894 Bass guided a young woman named Ada Diefendorf to the beautiful waterfalls in Havasu Canyon. A short while later, Bill and Ada were married, and Ada became the first white woman to raise a family on the South Rim. But life in Grand Canyon was never easy. In addition to household duties such as cooking and cleaning, Ada wrangled horses, cared for livestock, and hiked three days to do laundry in the Colorado River.

In 1926, at the age of 77, Bass sold the claims to his land holdings and retired to Wickenburg, Arizona. By the time he left, he had built more roads and Inner Canyon trails than any other individual in Grand Canyon history.

THE RAILROAD ARRIVES

MINERS AT THE rim weren't the only ones interested in a railroad to Grand Canyon. The nearby towns of Flagstaff and Williams also realized the benefits that a railroad would bring—namely increased tourist dollars—and both towns were soon engaged in a feverish competition to build one. Flagstaff envisioned a railroad supported by tourism. The town's leading citizens pitched their idea to a number of established railroad companies, but as Bill Bass had already discovered, the railroads failed to grasp Grand Canyon's tourism potential.

Williams took a different approach. The town appealed to mining companies who needed a cheap way to haul ore from their mines located near the South Rim. Mining operations would be the driving force for the new railroad, with tourist dollars providing additional revenue. It was a shrewd pitch, and in 1897 the Santa Fe and Grand Canyon Railway Company was incorporated to build a railroad connecting Williams to the South Rim.

Four years later, the railroad reached Grand Canyon Village. By that time, however, the mines that prompted its construction had already been shut down. It hardly mattered. For $3.95 passengers could enjoy a smooth, four-hour train ride to the South Rim instead of a $20, bouncing, all-day stage ride—previously the only option. The result was predictable: tourism boomed.

Visitors arrived by the thousands. The railroad flourished, and before long the price of land near Grand Canyon Village had skyrocketed. A few cunning locals staked bogus mining claims along the South Rim, giving them the questionable

All Rail to Grand Canyon

Of Arizona ; no stage ride ; Santa Fe trains to the rim.
The only scenery in America that comes up to its brag. Earth's armies could be lost in this stupendous gulf.
The chief attraction of a California tour.
Books about Grand Canyon and California, 10 cents.

Santa Fe

Gen. Pass. Office, A. T. & S. F. R'y, Chicago.

ARIZONA PROSPECTOR

right to develop the land. Although the practice was ultimately ruled illegal, a few citizens—most notably Ralph Cameron (p.83)—became rich off the scheme.

The Santa Fe Railroad owned most of the land surrounding its tracks, giving it a strategic advantage in the local real estate game. To accommodate the flood of new visitors, the railroad built the extravagant El Tovar hotel in Grand Canyon Village. Early settlers who had built hotels outside of Grand Canyon Village soon found it hard to compete. Within a decade, most locally owned hotels had shut down.

Life on the rim was changing fast. Just three months after the first train pulled up to the South Rim, the first automobile arrived. Its driver had departed from Flagstaff several days earlier amid much fanfare, but the car broke down soon after it left. Several days later, the automobile arrived at the South Rim pulled by a team of mules. Over the next three decades, however, automobiles would become the most popular form of transportation to Grand Canyon, ultimately forcing the railroad out of business.

While the South Rim buzzed with tourist activity, the North Rim remained as isolated as ever. No railroads came within 100 miles of the North Rim, and settlement was scare. Because of its extreme isolation, the Arizona Strip—the narrow stretch of land between the North Rim and Utah—was a lawless area that attracted a strange mix of cattle thieves, renegades, and Mormons who continued to practice polygamy. Although Utah tried several times to annex the Arizona Strip, citing Arizona's poor law enforcement as a primary concern, Arizona was able to retain control of the land.

Due to its remote location, the North Rim was also filled with wild game, a fact that soon attracted hunting parties. North Rim sport hunting got off to a rocky start, however, when a man named John Young attempted to build a hunting lodge that would cater to British aristocrats. Young contacted Buffalo Bill Cody, who was then performing in England, and convinced him to round up a group of potential investors. When the eager Britons arrived later that year, they took one look at the desolate landscape and hightailed it back to England.

American hunters, on the other hand, were more than happy to venture to the rugged North Rim, and sport hunting soon flourished. In 1906 Congress established Grand Canyon Game Reserve, which included much of the North Rim. A few years later, ex-President Theodore Roosevelt visited the North Rim on a hunting trip. Starting from the South Rim, he descended the Bright Angel Trail and boarded a metal cage that shuttled passengers across the river via a cable and pulley system. Halfway across the river, one of the cables snapped. The cage jolted violently, but Roosevelt made it safely across. After exiting the cage, Roosevelt was said to cry out, "Let's do it again!"

High-profile visits like these focused even greater attention on the region. It soon became clear that Grand Canyon was not just another tourist attraction, but a major national landmark. Many felt it deserved to be recognized as such. Before long, the wheels were in motion to create Grand Canyon National Park.

The South Rim
SWINDLER

OF ALL THE real estate swindlers who came to Grand Canyon in the late 1800s, none was more successful than Ralph Cameron. Shortly after the arrival of the railroad, Cameron began staking mining claims along the South Rim, and before long he had staked over 13,000 acres. But Cameron had little interest in mining. The claims gave him the right to develop the land, which was much more valuable as commercial real estate.

For his claims to be legal, however, he needed to actually mine the land. Cameron paid little attention to this technicality. He simply "salted" the claims with imported minerals and set up bogus mining equipment. Once his claims were established, Cameron took great pleasure in lording them over the Santa Fe Railroad, which felt *it* had the right to develop the land.

One of Cameron's most contentious claims was located next to the train depot, a spot where he knew the railroad wanted to build a hotel. Cameron built his own hotel there instead. In retaliation, the railroad moved their terminal several hundred feet to the east so train passengers would have to pass the railroad-owned Bright Angel Hotel on their way to Cameron's hotel. Visitation to Cameron's hotel soon plummeted.

But Cameron had one more trick up his sleeve. His "mining" claims also gave him sole control of the Bright Angel Trail, the only trail into the Canyon anywhere near Grand Canyon Village. Acting as tollkeeper, Cameron charged $1 a head for every tourist who wanted to descend the trail on horseback. The railroad filed a lawsuit, but Cameron prevailed in court. In retaliation, the railroad spent thousands of dollars improving the Hermit Trail, located several miles west of the Bright Angel Trail, as an alternative to the Bright Angel Trail. But Cameron, who owned mining claims on the Hermit Trail too, howled at the injustice. Tired of his antics, the railroad relented and paid him $40,000 for his bogus claims.

As the years wore on, Cameron lost the will to compete with the railroad. In 1910 he shut down his hotel, but he continued to charge a toll on the Bright Angel Trail. By the time the Park Service finally gained control of the trail, Cameron had leveraged his wealth and power into a seat in the U.S. Senate. For years he continued to fight the park over the legitimacy of his mining claims. It wasn't until 1920 that the Arizona Supreme Court finally invalidated Cameron's claims, ending his once-grand real estate empire.

John Hance & Teddy Roosevelt

Park Entrance, 1931

GRAND CANYON NATIONAL PARK

AS EARLY AS 1882, Indiana Senator Benjamin Harrison had introduced legislation to preserve Grand Canyon as a national park. At that time there was only one other national park—Yellowstone, created in 1872—but Harrison's legislation faltered in the face of opposition from local miners and ranchers. Harrison reintroduced legislation again in 1883 and 1886, but again the idea was shot down. Two decades later, when Harrison became President, he used his power to establish "Great Canyon Reserve." It was a victory for Grand Canyon, but many Arizona miners and cattlemen resented the new restrictions placed on the land.

Despite scattered local opposition, there were many who saw the need to protect Grand Canyon. In 1906 the Act for the Preservation of American Antiquities was passed, giving the President the power to set aside areas that held "objects of historic or scientific nature." That same year President Theodore Roosevelt created Grand Canyon Game Reserve. For Roosevelt it was an easy decision. When he had visited Grand Canyon a few years earlier, he proclaimed it to be "the most impressive scenery I have ever looked at."

The creation of Grand Canyon Game Reserve was just the beginning. Two years later, Roosevelt established Grand Canyon National Monument—the highest designation a piece of American land can receive without Congressional approval. At that point Arizona was not yet a state, so it had no Senators or

Congressmen to champion the creation of a national park. In 1912 Arizona was admitted to the Union, and in 1917 Representative Carl Hayden and Senator Henry Fountain of Arizona introduced legislation to create Grand Canyon National Park. On February 26, 1919, President Woodrow Wilson signed the bill into law.

But creating a national park and running it smoothly were two different matters. Early administrators lacked a coherent vision for the park, and many major infrastructure issues went unresolved. In its first decade of operation, Grand Canyon National Park went through six superintendents. The park needed a strong leader with a long-term commitment to Grand Canyon. It found that leader in Miner Tillotson, a civil engineer who became superintendent in 1927 and occupied the position for over a decade. Through his tireless efforts, he helped shape a coherent vision of the park that set the precedent for years to come.

The same year that Tillotson became superintendent, Congress revised the park's boundaries to include a large portion of Kaibab National Forest. Five years later, President Herbert Hoover proclaimed a new Grand Canyon National Monument (the old one had become Grand Canyon National Park) that encompassed 300 square miles in western Grand Canyon and an additional 40 miles along the Colorado River.

The park was a success on paper, but the flood of new visitors soon overwhelmed the staff. In its first year as a national park, Grand Canyon received 44,000 visitors. Within a decade, that number rose to nearly 200,000. In 1937, 300,000 arrived. The numbers kept on climbing, but the park's staff remained the same: 10 rangers and one park superintendent. For years the small, dedicated staff worked long hours to accommodate the huge number of visitors. Ultimately, the number of rangers was increased, making the park much more enjoyable for both tourists and employees alike.

THE GREAT DAM WARS

BY THE 1960S, Grand Canyon seemed to be doing just fine. Its dedicated staff welcomed millions of people from around the world. Movie stars, British royalty, and Arab sheiks all stopped by for a look. The giant hole in the ground that had been avoided for centuries was now one of America's most cherished natural landmarks. Best of all, Grand Canyon's national park status protected it from private development. But a massive government project soon threatened to drastically alter the landscape.

In the early 1960s, the U.S. Bureau of Reclamation (the government agency responsible for much of the water supply in the West) went looking for a new place to build a dam. Ever since the overwhelming success of Hoover Dam, the Bureau had been constructing massive dams at a frantic rate. The West was growing fast, and it needed water to grow. In the 1930s, '40s, and '50s, the Bureau

of Reclamation built giant dams wherever it could. Before long, many of the Southwest's most impressive rivers resembled a string of interconnected reservoirs. By the early 1960s, there was only one good place left in America to build a giant dam: Grand Canyon.

With its steep walls, deep side canyons, and powerful river, Grand Canyon was the perfect site for a dam. But there was a catch: any reservoir created by a dam would be utterly impractical from a water-use standpoint. The water would have to be pumped out thousands of feet to bring it to civilization, and the costs involved would be prohibitively expensive. But the Bureau of Reclamation wasn't interested in water. It was interested in hydroelectricity. In effect, a dam in Grand Canyon would be nothing more than a giant cash register to fund other, less economically feasible water projects elsewhere. And the Bureau of Reclamation didn't just want one dam in the Grand Canyon. It wanted two.

When conservationists heard the news, they went wild. Conservationists detest dams, a fact that became apparent in 1948 when the Bureau of Reclamation tried to build a dam along the Green River in Echo Park, Utah. The dam would have flooded part of Dinosaur National Monument, and conservationists were loath to let that happen. Led by David Brower of the Sierra Club, they fought tooth and nail to defeat the dam. They succeeded. But their success came at a huge cost.

As part of the compromise to save Dinosaur National Monument, the two sides agreed upon a new dam farther downstream. The site of the new dam was Glen Canyon. Lying just north of Grand Canyon, Glen Canyon was one of the most remote places in the country. Only a few thousand people had ever seen it. So shortly before Glen Canyon Dam was finished, David Brower—the man who championed its creation—took a river trip through Glen Canyon to see it for himself. He immediately started to cry.

With its gorgeous sandstone arches, fern covered alcoves, and sweeping river views, Glen Canyon was one of the most beautiful places Brower had ever seen. In a few months, it would all be underwater. Brower would later admit that the creation of Glen Canyon Dam was the greatest failure of his life. From that moment

FLOYD DOMINY

"I like Dave Brower, but I don't think he's the sanctified conservationist that so many people think he is. I think he's a selfish preservationist, for the few. Dave Brower hates my guts. Why? Because I've got guts. I've tangled with Dave Brower for many years."

on, he vowed never again to lose another beautiful place to a dam. When Brower found out that the Bureau of Reclamation wanted to build two more dams in the Grand Canyon, he went into overdrive.

Brower was up against stiff competition. The biggest proponent of the new dams was Floyd Dominy, the head of the Bureau of Reclamation. Dominy had spent much of his early career helping struggling Wyoming ranchers build dams to save their families from poverty. He knew firsthand how a lack of water could lead to suffering, and he made it his life's mission to build dams. Dominy's drive and ambition were unprecedented. By the time he became head of the Bureau of Reclamation, he had many powerful allies, including Arizona Senator Carl Hayden, the chairman of the Appropriations Committee.

Brower versus Dominy. Conservation versus economic growth. The battle over the dams in Grand Canyon soon became much more than a battle for Grand Canyon. It became a battle for the future of environmental policy in America. For decades economic development had taken precedent over wilderness. But wilderness was disappearing fast, and many people wanted to preserve what was left before it was too late.

Debate over the dams soon shifted into the public arena. Defending the proposed dams, the Bureau of Reclamation argued that the reservoirs would help tourists enjoy Grand Canyon more fully by allowing them to explore previously inaccessible reaches of the Canyon from motorboats. In response, the Sierra Club took out full-page ads in the *New York Times*, *Los Angeles Times*, *San Francisco Chronicle*, and *Washington Post*. The ads read: "Should we also flood the Sistine Chapel so tourists can get nearer the ceiling?"

The response was overwhelming. Letters protesting the dams arrived at the Bureau of Reclamation in dump trucks. Senators and Congressmen were flooded with requests to save Grand Canyon. The two dams, which would have flooded much of Marble Canyon and the Lower Granite Gorge—including Havasu Creek, one of the most beautiful locations in the Canyon—were stopped dead in their tracks.

DAVID BROWER

"Lake Powell is a drag strip for power boats. It's for people who won't do things except the easy way. The magic of Glen Canyon is dead. It has been vulgarized. Putting water in the Cathedral in the Desert was like urinating on the crypt of St. Peter's."

GRAND CANYON TODAY

TODAY THE BIGGEST challenge facing Grand Canyon is the park's overwhelming number of visitors. In 1956 one million people visited Grand Canyon. Thirteen years later, that number doubled. Twenty years later it tripled. To cope with increased traffic and pollution, the park service closed Hermit Road to private vehicles in 1974 and began and offering a free shuttle instead. To deal with overcrowding below the rim, the park instituted a permit and reservation system for overnight camping. Before the permit system, it was not unusual for hundreds of people to camp at Phantom Ranch at the bottom of the Canyon—a place that can comfortably accommodate about 90 people.

To cope with increased visitation in the future, the National Park Service drafted a General Management Plan to reduce human impact on the park and keep Grand Canyon in as natural a state as possible. Under the plan, which will be instituted over time, private cars will not be allowed over much of the South Rim and visitors will be shuttled around entirely by bus or a proposed light rail system. Extensive "Greenway Trails" have also been built along the rim for bikers and pedestrians.

Today over four million people visit Grand Canyon each year. Those numbers are both a blessing and a challenge. But as long as every visitor makes a conscious effort to appreciate and preserve Grand Canyon, it will remain one of the world's great destinations for generations to come.

THE SOUTH RIM

★ ★ ★ ★ ★

THE SOUTH RIM

MASSIVE CLIFFS, TERRIFYING depths, soaring condors—these are just a few of the things you'll encounter at the South Rim, the most famous and popular part of the park. Perched a mile above the Colorado River at one of the widest spots in Grand Canyon, the South Rim is home to most of the park's lodges, campgrounds, and restaurants. Because of its proximity to Interstate 40, which runs through Flagstaff and Williams, the South Rim is the most accessible—and therefore most crowded—part of the park. But no matter how crowded it gets in the busy summer months, the views are always worth it. And between March and July, the South Rim is the easiest and most reliable place in the world to view California condors (p.46), one of the rarest and most magnificent birds in the world.

The South Rim is divided into three main areas: Grand Canyon Village (p.110), Hermit Road (p.128), and Desert View Drive (p.146), all of which provide access to dramatic viewpoints and great hikes. To help reduce traffic, the park offers a free shuttle connecting lodges, park buildings, and popular viewpoints in Grand Canyon Village and along Hermit Road. Between March 1 and November 30, Hermit Road is closed to private vehicle traffic, but you can still explore its sights on foot or by bike. To explore Desert View Drive, which heads 25 miles east of Grand Canyon Village to Desert View, you can either drive your own car or purchase a ticket for a narrated bus tour (p.107).

Grand Canyon Village (elevation 6,800 feet) is the hub of all tourist activity on the South Rim. Its five lodges—the only lodges on the South Rim—accommodate about 1,000 guests, and nearby services include everything from fine dining to auto repair. Grand Canyon Village is also the jumping off point for narrated bus tours and mule trips along popular trails (p.107), as well as the meeting spot for many of the park's excellent, free ranger programs (p.107).

Other than the easy Rim Trail (p.103), which skirts the edge of the Canyon near Grand Canyon Village, hiking on the South Rim is limited to a handful of trails that drop down the Canyon's steep walls. Hiking from the rim to the Colorado River and back in a single day is very dangerous (some hikers have died in their attempts), but day hikers can still get a sense of the Inner Canyon's beauty by descending only partway down popular trails. The Bright Angel Trail (p.168) is the South Rim's most famous (and crowded) hike, but the South Kaibab Trail (p.178), Hermit Trail (p.184) and Grandview Trail (p.190) offer equally dramatic scenery with fewer crowds.

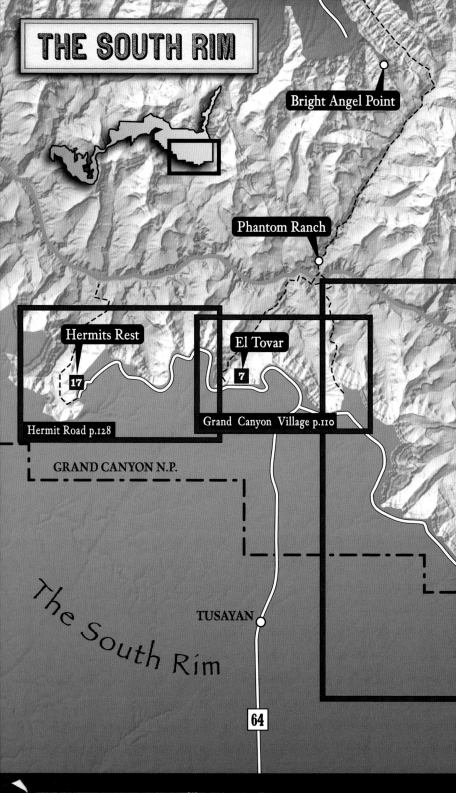

The North Rim

N

Cape Royal

Desert View

23

64

Desert View Drive

Desert View Drive p.146

One Perfect Day on the South Rim

- Sunrise at Mather Point (p.113)
- Breakfast at Bright Angel Restaurant (p.106)
- Check out native crafts at Hopi House (p.119)
- Walk the Trail of Time to Yavapai Point (p.118)
- Explore the Yavapai Geology Museum (p.115)
- Buy sandwiches at Canyon Village Deli (p.106)
- Drive to Shoshone Point for a picnic lunch (p.153)
- Drive to Tusayan Ruin (p.161)
- Drive to Desert View (p.164)
- Sunset at Hopi Point (p.134)
- Dinner at El Tovar (p.106)

Another Perfect Day on the South Rim

- Sunrise at Maricopa Point (p.130)
- Breakfast at Bright Angel Restaurant (p.106)
- Morning mule ride along the rim (p.107)
- Lunch at El Tovar (p.106)
- Early afternoon scenic flight (p.23)
- Afternoon ranger condor talk (p.107)
- Cocktails at El Tovar (p.106)
- Sunset at Yavapai Point (p.115)
- Dinner at Arizona Room (p.106)

South Rim
BASICS

Getting to the South Rim

BY CAR

If you're traveling from Flagstaff or Williams, the most direct route to the South Rim heads north on AZ–64, past the small towns of Valle and Tusayan to Grand Canyon's South Entrance Station (about 60 miles north of I-40). An alternate route follows US–180 from Flagstaff past the dramatic San Francisco Peaks to Valle, where US–180 merges with AZ–64. If you're driving from northeast Arizona, enter the park via the eastern stretch of AZ–64. From US–89, follow AZ–64 to the East Entrance Station, about 25 miles east of Grand Canyon Village.

BY BUS

Free Shuttles, offered by the National Park Service, run between the town of Tusayan and the South Rim Visitor Center in the summer. Note: To ride this shuttle you must have a valid park entrance permit, available for purchase at the National Geographic Visitor Center in Tusayan.

Arizona Shuttle (877-226-8060, www.arizonashuttle.com) offers daily shuttle service from Flagstaff and Williams to the South Rim ($25 one-way). **Transcanyon Shuttle** (928-638-2820, www.trans-canyonshuttle.com) offers a daily shuttle between the South Rim and North Rim ($85 one-way). **Flagstaff Shuttle** (888-215-3105, www.flagshuttle.com) offers chartered shuttles to the South Rim from Flagstaff, Sedona, Phoenix and Las Vegas.

BY TRAIN

Grand Canyon Railway (800-843-8724, www.thetrain.com) offers daily train service between Williams and Grand Canyon Village in vintage railroad cars. The 65-mile trip takes a little over two hours, arriving at 11:45am and departing at 3:30pm. Overnight package deals with lodging are available.

BY PLANE

The two closest major airports to the South Rim are **McCarran International Airport** in Las Vegas and **Phoenix Sky Harbor International Airport**. Phoenix is about 220 miles from the South Rim; Las Vegas is about 290 miles from the South Rim. A handful of commercial carriers fly into **Pulliam Airport** in Flagstaff, Arizona. Grand Canyon Airlines (866-235-9422, www.grandcanyonairlines.com) offers flights to tiny **Grand Canyon Airport** in Tusayan (p.108) from Boulder City, Nevada, near Las Vegas.

Fees

The South Rim entrance fee (which also gives you access to the North Rim) is $25 per vehicle or $12 per pedestrian, motorcycle rider or cyclist. This pass is good for seven days and includes both rims. There's also an annual pass to Grand Canyon ($50) and the America The Beautiful Pass ($80), which gives you unlimited access to all U.S. national parks and federal recreation lands for one full year.

Information

The best source of seasonal Grand Canyon information—shuttle times, ranger programs—is the park's free newspaper, *The Guide*, which is available at all entrance stations, visitor centers, and lodges. A PDF version of the guide can be downloaded at the park's official website: www.nps.gov/grca. The park's Twitter feed, @GrandCanyonNPS, is a great resource for weather updates and park alerts.

The Grand Canyon Visitor Center (p.112) is the park's premier information resource. Ranger-staffed information desks are also found at Yavapai Geology Museum (p.115), Verkamp's Visitor Center (p.118), Kolb Studio (p.127), Tusayan Museum (p.161), and Desert View (p.164).

Transportation Desks with information on mule rides, air tours and motor tours are located in Bright Angel Lodge, Maswik Lodge and Yavapai Lodge. The South Rim's Backcountry Information Center, where backpackers can inquire about permits and trail conditions, is located behind Maswik Lodge.

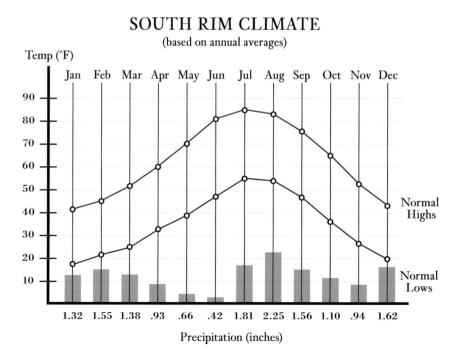

SOUTH RIM CLIMATE
(based on annual averages)

Weather & When to Go

SPRING

This is one of the best times to visit the South Rim. In general, temperatures are mild, precipitation is light, and the crowds are manageable. Early spring is also a great time to hike the South Rim's Inner Canyon trails, which are hot and uncomfortable in the summer. By June daily highs on the South Rim can top 80°F, but snowfall has been recorded as late as mid-June. Spring is also wildflower season, although the intensity of the blooms depends upon the amount of precipitation that fell in the winter. Some years the blooms are spectacular; other years they are far less dramatic.

SUMMER

This is the most popular time to visit, but the large crowds, hot temperatures, and late-summer thunderstorms all combine to make summer a less than ideal time to visit. Despite these minor annoyances, the view from the rim remains spectacular, and a thunderstorm over Grand Canyon is an amazing sight to behold. Thunderstorms are most common during "monsoon season," which lasts from July through mid-September. Also be aware that scorching midday temperatures in the Inner Canyon make many of the park's popular hiking trails unbearable in July and August. Phantom Ranch, at the bottom of Grand Canyon, has recorded summer highs of 120°F!

FALL

Fall is a terrific time to visit Grand Canyon. The crowds drop off dramatically after Labor Day, and the climate starts to dry out after the summer monsoons end, usually around mid-September. As the days grow shorter, the Canyon is bathed in gorgeous autumn light. Like spring, fall is a great time to hike the South Rim's Inner Canyon trails due to milder temperatures and reduced crowds. Fall weather can be unpredictable, however, so be sure to bring plenty of warm cloths and rain gear. By mid-October, nighttime temperatures usually start dropping below freezing along the South Rim.

WINTER

In my opinion, winter is the most underrated time to visit Grand Canyon. Yes, you'll contend with daily highs in the 40s and freezing temperatures at night, but winter also means minimal crowds, reduced rates at park lodges, and the possibility of snow. The South Rim averages about five feet of snow each winter, and if you're lucky enough to visit during a snowstorm you'll witness Grand Canyon at its most beautiful. Although you'll need to bundle up in warm clothes on the rim, the bottom of the Canyon often experiences spring-like temperatures in late winter, making this a great time to spend the night at Phantom Ranch (p.177) or Bright Angel Campground (p.105).

Getting Around the South Rim

BY CAR

Exploring the South Rim in your own car lets you hop from sight to sight at your own pace, but traffic and parking can be a significant hassle during the busy summer months. Furthermore, Hermit Road and the road to Yaki Point are closed to private vehicle traffic from March through November. But no matter what time of year you visit, it's generally best to park your car and use the park's free shuttle system. You'll still need a car to explore Desert View Drive, which is not serviced by the shuttles, though there is a narrated 4-hour bus tour (p.107).

BY SHUTTLE

To reduce traffic and pollution, the park offers free shuttles between popular South Rim destinations. The three major shuttle routes service Grand Canyon Village, Hermit Road and the South Kaibab trailhead. A seasonal shuttle services the town of Tusayan. Routes and schedules vary from season to season, so pick up a copy of *The Guide* for the most up-to-date shuttle information.

BY BICYCLE

Bicycles are permitted on all paved park roads, but dealing with car traffic can be a pain, especially during the busy summer months. Fortunately, the South Rim has over 12 miles of Greenway Trails, which are paved roads open exclusively to bicyclists, hikers and wheelchair users. Greenway Trails radiate out from the Grand Canyon Visitor Center (p.112) to Grand Canyon Village (p.110), the South Kaibab Trailhead (p.178), and the town of Tusayan (p.108). There are also three miles of Greenway Trails along Hermit Road (p.128) between Monument Creek Vista and Hermits Rest. If you don't have your own bike, Bright Angel Bicycles (928-814-8704, www.bikegrandcanyon.com), located at the Grand Canyon Visitor Center (p.112), offers bike rentals and guided tours. In addition, all of the park's free shuttles are equipped with bicycle racks.

ON FOOT VIA THE RIM TRAIL

Wheels are great, but I believe hiking is still the best way to take in the Grand Canyon, slowing down the pace so you can soak in the magnificent scenery. The easy, 12-mile Rim Trail skirts the rim of the Canyon from Hermit's Rest to Pipe Creek Vista, passing by many of the South Rim's most famous viewpoints along the way. Because park shuttles service many of those viewpoints, you can hike for as little or as long as you'd like, then simply hop on a shuttle. Although the Rim Trail is often crowded near popular viewpoints, the stretches between viewpoints offer good opportunities for solitude. The Rim Trail also has a fantastic new geology exhibit, the Trail of Time (p.118), which is walking timeline of Earth history that stretches 2.8 miles between Yavapai Point and Verkamp's Visitor Center.

Lodging

All South Rim hotels are run by **Xanterra Parks and Resorts**. Rooms fill up fast, so book your reservations as far in advance as possible, especially for the busy summer months. Rates listed below are based on the busy summer season; winter rates are often much cheaper. (888-297-2757, www.grandcanyonlodges.com)

★ EL TOVAR HOTEL

This historic hotel (p.120), first opened in 1905, offers the most luxurious lodging in Grand Canyon. If you've got the cash, there's no better place to stay. Perched right on the rim, several rooms at El Tovar have Canyon views. But rooms are often booked months in advance. **Rates:** $180–$280

★ BRIGHT ANGEL LODGE & CABINS

This rustic hotel, perched next to the rim of the Canyon (p.124), has a bit of a split personality. Its basic rooms (no private bath, showers down the hall) offer some of the best budget lodging in the park, while its premium rooms and private cabins feature sweeping Canyon views and working fireplaces. **Rates:** $70–$185

★ PHANTOM RANCH

This fantastic collection of rustic buildings, nestled at the bottom of the Canyon along Bright Angel Creek, offers the only overnight lodging below the rim. See page 181 for further details. **Rates:** $46-$150

KACHINA & THUNDERBIRD LODGES

These blocky, utilitarian buildings, set about 60 feet back from the rim, are situated between Bright Angel Lodge and El Tovar. Surprisingly, there's not much in the way of Canyon views, but the central location is a big plus. Both lodges offer standard motel-style rooms with two queen beds. **Rates:** $180–$190

MASWIK LODGE

Set a quarter-mile back from the rim, Maswik Lodge offers basic motel-style rooms with two queen beds. The lodge is divided into north and south sections (rooms in the north section are more spacious and offer more amenities). In the summer, small rustic cabins are also available. The cabins feature two queen-size (or two double beds) and a private shower. **Rates:** $90–175

YAVAPAI LODGE

Yavapai Lodge is the largest lodge in the park, but because it's situated a half mile from the rim it's less popular than other lodges. That said, it's also the most likely to have rooms on short notice. The lodge offers standard motel-style rooms at Yavapai East (air conditioning) and Yavapai West (ceiling fans). **Rates:** $123–165

Camping on the South Rim

MATHER CAMPGROUND

Nestled in a ponderosa forest near Grand Canyon Village, this large campground has over 300 campsites and is open year-round. Each campsite accommodates up to six people, three tents and two vehicles. (No RV hook-ups, 30-foot max. vehicle length.) Coin-operated hot showers and laundry are available. Cost: $18 per campsite per night. Reservations, which are highly recommended April–October, can be made up to six months in advance (www.recreation.gov, 800-444-6777).

TRAILER VILLAGE

Located next to Mather Campground, this popular RV campground offers RV hook-ups for vehicles up to 50 feet in length. Open year-round. Cost: $35. Reservations highly recommended April–October. Call 888-297-2757 for advance reservations; 928-638-2631 for same-day reservations.

DESERT VIEW CAMPGROUND

This campground, located 26 miles east of Grand Canyon Village at Desert View (p.164), is open early May through mid-October. The 50 campsites are available on a first-come, first-served basis, and each site accommodates up to six people, three tents and two vehicles. No showers, laundry or RV hook-ups. Cost: $12 per campsite per night

Inner Canyon Camping

Two popular campgrounds are located below the rim, but they are only accessible on foot or by mule. Both campgrounds offer restrooms and running water. Reservations are issued as permits by the Backcountry Office (p.13).

INDIAN GARDEN CAMPGROUND

Located 4.6 miles down the popular Bright Angel Trail, Indian Garden Campground sits above the lush banks of Garden Creek, which supports a thriving population of shady cottonwood trees.

BRIGHT ANGEL CAMPGROUND

This charming campground, located at the bottom of the Canyon between the Colorado River and Phantom Ranch, is accessible via the Bright Angel Trail or the South Kaibab Trail. The campground is situated just above the banks of Bright Angel Creek, and each of the 32 campsites comes with a picnic table and fire ring. If you don't want to lug your gear up or down the Canyon, arrange for a mule to carry up to 30 pounds of gear ($67 one-way); call 888-297-2757 for more information about mule "Duffel Service."

Dining

Almost all South Rim restaurants are located in Grand Canyon Village (the lone exception is a small snackbar at Desert View). During the busy summer months, restaurants that don't accept reservations fill up fast, and waiting times can sometimes exceed two hours. Tip: If you want to beat the crowds, plan on arriving before sunset.

★ EL TOVAR DINING ROOM (Brk: $9-12; Lnch: $11–16; Din: $18–30)

For over 100 years, the El Tovar Dining Room has offered the finest dining on the South Rim. Not surprisingly, it's also the most expensive restaurant, but the soft lighting, dark wood paneling, and elegant/rustic atmosphere are definitely worth it. Reservations are required for dinner, and they are available up to six months in advance. (928-638-2631 x6432)

★ ARIZONA ROOM (Lnch: $9–13, Din: $18–28)

After El Tovar, this is your best bet for dinner on the South Rim. Located in the Bright Angel Lodge, it serves steakhouse favorites and Southwestern fare. The atmosphere is nice—especially the large picture windows with views of the rim. Reservations are not accepted, so arrive early to beat the crowds.

BRIGHT ANGEL RESTAURANT (Brk $6–8; Lnch: $8–10, Din: $9–16)

The third best restaurant on the South Rim offers steakhouse favorites, Southwestern specialties, and some salad and veggie options. No reservations.

CANYON VILLAGE DELI (Brk: $3–5; Lnch: $6–8)

This is your best bet for healthy, inexpensive take-out sandwiches. Located in the General Store.

MASWIK PIZZA PUB (Pizza: $13–18; Slices: $2.50–3)

Fresh-baked pizza, wings, draft beer and sports on TV. Located in Maswik Lodge adjacent to the cafeteria.

MASWIK CAFETERIA (Brk: $4–7; Lnch, Din: $7–10)

Cafeteria-style food. Located in Maswik Lodge.

YAVAPAI CAFETERIA (Brk: $4–7; Lnch, Din: $7–10)

Cafeteria-style food. Located in Yavapai Lodge.

Cocktails

EL TOVAR LOUNGE (11am–11pm)

This is the best place to enjoy a drink on the South Rim. Not only can you soak in El Tovar's sumptuous surroundings, there's an outdoor patio with views of the rim. Draft beer, wine, creative cocktails, light appetizers.

Activities

RANGER PROGRAMS

Free ranger programs are offered throughout the year, and they are one of the best ways to learn about the fascinating natural and human history of Grand Canyon. Among the most popular are Geology Talks, Fossil Walks, California Condor Talks, and the evening program at the Shrine of the Ages auditorium. Ranger programs generally last 30–60 minutes, and they are offered throughout the day. Check *The Guide* for seasonal times and locations.

BUS TOURS

Xanterra (888-297-2757, www.grandcanyonlodges.com) offers narrated bus tours along the South Rim, all of which depart from Grand Canyon Village. The **Desert View Tour** (4 hours, $47) heads east along Desert View Drive. The **Hermit Road Tour** (2 hours, $28) travels west along Hermit Drive. Sunrise and sunset tours (1.5 hours, $22) also run May–October, and a package deal offering two tours is available for $40. Children under 16 ride for free. For more information, contact the transportation desk at Bright Angel Lodge, Maswik Lodge, or Yavapai Lodge.

MULE RIDES

Both day and overnight mule rides depart daily from the South Rim. The 3-hour **Canyon Vistas Mule Ride** ($114) heads east of Yaki Point along the newly constructed East Rim Trail. Trips depart at 9am and 1pm. **Overnight Mule Rides** follow the Bright Angel Trail to the bottom of Grand Canyon, where riders spend the night at Phantom Ranch (p.177), then return the next day via the South Kaibab Trail ($507 for one person, $895 for two people). Rides offering an extra night at Phantom Ranch are also available ($714 for one person, $1,192 for two people). Due to the popularity of Mule Rides, reservations should be made as soon as possible (they are accepted up to one year in advance). Contact Xanterra for additional information (888-297-2757, www.grandcanyonlodges.com). See page 17 for more information on mule rides in Grand Canyon.

GRAND CANYON STAR PARTY

Grand Canyon boasts some of the darkest skies left in the continental U.S., and local astronomy clubs celebrate this fact each June by setting up telescopes for the public on the South Rim. Exact dates vary depending on the new moon.

GRAND CANYON MUSIC FESTIVAL

This popular festival features concerts in late August and early September at the Shrine of the Ages auditorium. (www.grandcanyonmusicfest.org)

ART EXHIBITS

Kolb Studio (127) features regularly changing art exhibits.

TUSAYAN

The tiny town of Tusayan (144 acres, pop. 558) is located 1.5 miles south of the national park's South Entrance Station. Sandwiched between Grand Canyon National Park to the north and the Kaibab National Forest to the south, it's the only private property anywhere near the South Rim's popular sights. As such, Tusayan revolves entirely around Grand Canyon tourism, and its commercial district along highway 64 is packed with hotels, restaurants and the area's only gas station. Just south of the commercial district is Grand Canyon Airport, which services sightseeing flights (p.23) and private planes. Note: From Tusayan to the Grand Canyon Visitor Center it's about a 15-minute drive.

Lodging & Camping

Lodging in Tusayan is often more expensive than lodging in the park because many of the town's hotels offer luxuries such as swimming pools, spas and other modern amenities. But when all the park hotels are booked, Tusayan is your only lodging option anywhere near the South Rim. Tusayan camping options include the private Grand Canyon Camper Village and the Ten X Campground, two miles south of Tusayan in the Kaibab National Forest. For a complete list of Tusayan hotels and campgrounds visit www.jameskaiser.com.

Dining

Dining options in Tusayan are limited to fast food chains and restaurants catering to tourists. Try your luck at the following places.

YIPPEI-EI-O! STEAKHOUSE (Lnch, Din: $14-24)
This cowboy-themed restaurant serves steaks and ribs cooked over juniper wood, plus some vegetarian options. Try the rattlesnake appetizer. (928-638-2780)

SOPHIE'S MEXICAN KITCHEN (Lnch, Din: $11-17)
If you're feeling like Mexican head to Sophie's, which features all the classics: tacos, burritos, fajitas, enchiladas, tostadas, tamales. (928-638-4654)

CANYON STAR (Brk, Lnch: $9-14; Din: $17–26)
Located in The Grand Hotel, Canyon Star offers Southwestern fare (steaks, ribs) plus burgers, soups, salads. The bar has a large beer selection. (928-638-3333)

CORONADO DINING ROOM (Brk, Lnch: $8-10; Din: $23–29)
Located in the Best Western, the menu is heavy on steakhouse favorites, including local specialties like elk. (928-638-2681)

WE COOK PIZZA AND PASTA (Lnch, Din: $9-20)
Serves—you guessed it—pizza and pasta. (928-638-2278)

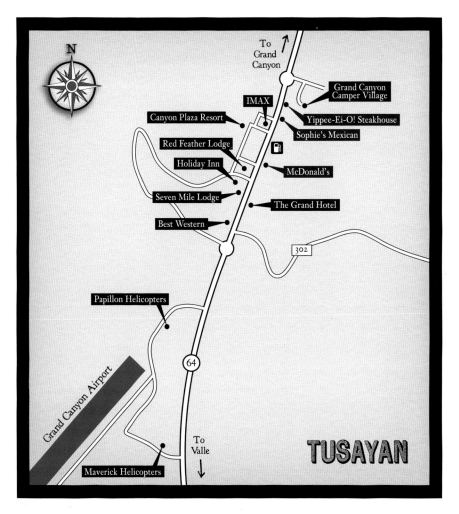

Entertainment

IMAX THEATER

Year after year, the IMAX film *Grand Canyon—The Hidden Secrets* lures hordes of visitors to its 70-foot screen. Short of going on a two-week river trip, this is a great way to check out some of Grand Canyon's most spectacular scenery. The 35-minute movie plays every hour on the half hour. Cost: $12.50 adults, $11.50 seniors & military, $9.50 children. (928-638-2468, www.explorethecanyon.com)

APACHE STABLES

Located one mile north of Tusayan, Apache Stables offers one- and two-hour horseback rides through the Kaibab National Forest during the day and campfire wagon rides in the evening. (928-638-2891, www.apachestables.com)

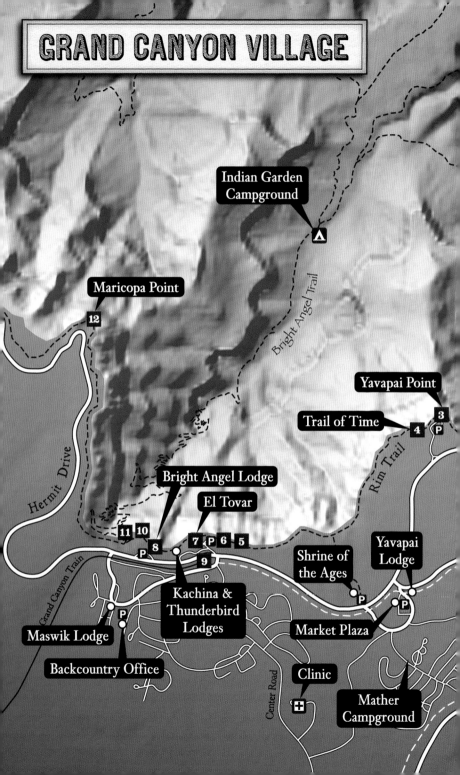

GRAND CANYON VILLAGE

Indian Garden
Campground

Maricopa Point

12

Yavapai Point

Trail of Time

3
P

4

Bright Angel Lodge

El Tovar

Rim Trail

Bright Angel Trail

Hermit Drive

11 10

8

P

7 P 6 5

9

Shrine of
the Ages

P

Yavapai
Lodge

P

Kachina &
Thunderbird
Lodges

Market Plaza

P

Grand Canyon Train

P

Maswik Lodge

P

Backcountry Office

Center Road

Clinic

Mather
Campground

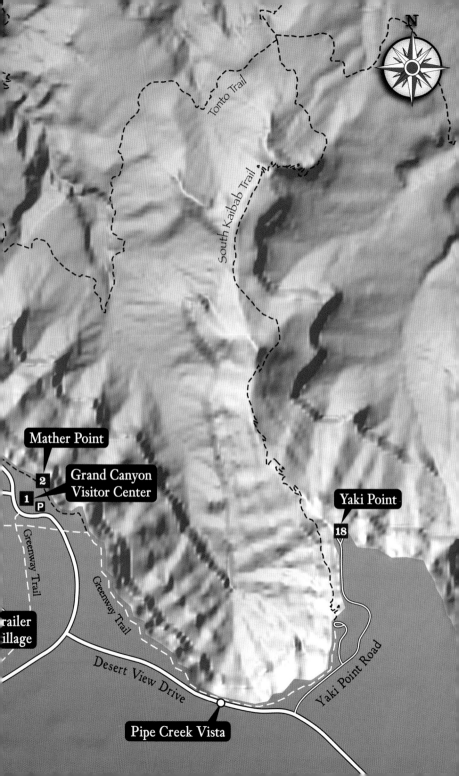

1 Grand Canyon Visitor Center

This cluster of buildings is Grand Canyon's main visitor center, and it should be one of your first stops upon entering the park. The main visitor center features a ranger-staffed information desk and interesting exhibits. Outside panels offer a wealth of additional information on everything from hiking to geology. A free 20-minute film, *Grand Canyon: A Journey of Wonder*, is shown every hour and half-hour between 8:30am and 4:30pm. Directly across the way is the Visitor Center Park Store, a terrific shop operated by the non-profit Grand Canyon Association that sells books, maps and gifts. Next door, Bright Angel Bicycles rents bicycles and sells coffee, wraps and sandwiches at their small café.

If you're only visiting the South Rim for the day, consider parking at the Visitor Center and exploring the South Rim via the park's free shuttle system. Parking is limited along the South Rim, and finding parking spaces can be hard, especially during the peak summer months. Both the Village Route Shuttle (which services Grand Canyon Village) and the Kaibab Rim Route Shuttle (which services Yavapai Point, Yaki Point and the South Kaibab Trailhead) make regular stops at the Grand Canyon Visitor Center.

Another great way to explore the South Rim without the hassle of driving is renting bicycles from Bright Angel Bicycles. The South Rim has over 12 miles of paved, automobile-free Greenway Trails perfect for biking, and the park's free shuttle buses come equipped with bicycle racks. See page 103 for more information about the park's Greenway Trails.

2 Mather Point

Mather Point is the most popular viewpoint in the park—a fact due mostly to its proximity to the South Rim Visitor Center. Still, the views here are great. As you stare out at the cascade of rock forms, ponder the fact that only one-third of the total length of the Grand Canyon is visible from Mather Point. At 277 miles, Grand Canyon is roughly *one-tenth* the length of the continental United States. But is it the largest canyon on Earth? Technically, over a dozen other canyons are deeper or wider or longer. But no other canyon on Earth is as deep *and* wide *and* long *and* geologically dramatic as Grand Canyon. (That said, Valles Marineris on Mars is nine time longer, seven times deeper, and 37 times wider than Grand Canyon, making it the largest canyon in the solar system!)

Mather Point is often one of the busiest spots in the park, especially during peak season. Keep in mind that there are equally fantastic viewpoints nearby, so if the crowds are overwhelming don't hesitate to move on to, say, Yavapai Point just down the road. Remember: You can always come back to Mather Point later.

Mather Point is named for Stephen Mather, a wealthy industrialist who made his fortune mining borax in Death Valley. In 1914 Mather complained to Interior Secretary Franklin Lane about the management of America's national parks. Lane's response: "If you don't like the way the national parks are being run, come on down to Washington and run them yourself." Mather did just that, becoming the first director of the National Park Service and spending the next 13 years shaping a strong, enduring vision for America's national parks.

③ Yavapai Point

This dramatic viewpoint juts out relatively far into the Canyon, providing some of the best views on the South Rim. Visitors can see over a dozen prominent landmarks, which is why the park service created Grand Canyon's first museum here in 1928. The current Yavapai Geology Museum remains one of the best places to learn about the park's geology. Inside you'll find fascinating exhibits on everything from the formation of rock layers to the carving of Grand Canyon by the Colorado River. Large viewing windows offer sweeping panoramas, making this a great place to take shelter on cold winter days or during summer thunderstorms. At sunrise and sunset, savvy visitors flock to Yavapai Point for its relatively clear views east and west.

One of the most prominent sights from Yavapai Point is Bright Angel Canyon, which slices eight miles into the North Rim. The North Kaibab Trail (p.274) runs through much of Bright Angel Canyon, and as the trail nears the Colorado River it passes by Phantom Ranch (p.177), a collection of small buildings offering the only overnight lodging at the bottom of Grand Canyon. Yavapai Point is one of the few places on the South Rim with views of Phantom Ranch (look for the faint patch of trees near the head of Bright Angel Canyon). Another famous feature visible from Yavapai Point is the broad, flat Tonto Platform, located just above the dark Inner Gorge near the bottom of the Canyon. Eagle-eyed visitors can spot the faint Tonto Trail running east-west along the Tonto Platform south of the Colorado River.

"It seems a gigantic statement for even nature to make, all in one mighty stone word, apprehended at once like a burst of light ... Wildness so godful, cosmic, primeval, bestows a new sense of earth's beauty and size."

—John Muir

View near Yavapai Point

Welcome to the Trail of Time,
a geology timeline.

4 Trail of Time

This walking timeline of Earth history in Grand Canyon is a geologist's dream
come true. Each meter represents one million years, so the 1.3 miles (2.1 km) trail
between Yavapai Geology Museum and Verkamp's Visitor Center represents 2.1
billion years of Earth history. Nothing puts Grand Canyon's age in perspective
like a stroll down the Trail of Time. The official start of the trail is located just
west of the Yavapai Geology Museum, but the trail is equally fascinating starting from Verkamp's. Bronze markers embedded in the path mark your location,
and a series of exhibits discuss key aspects of Grand Canyon's geology along the
way. The opening/closing exhibits, which display Grand Canyon's rock layers, are
constructed from actual rocks taken from the depths of the Canyon.

5 Verkamp's Visitor Center

At the western end of the Trail of Time you'll find this charming visitor center,
which is home to an information desk, bookstore and exhibits about Grand
Canyon's early pioneer days. The building was originally operated as "Verkamp's
Curios" by John G. Verkamp, a Grand Canyon pioneer who sold "curios" (unique
gifts) to early tourists. After Verkamp's death, his descendents carried on the
family tradition until 2008, when the National Park Service acquired the building. That ended the Verkamp family's 103-year streak as the longest family-owned
business in the national park system.

6 Hopi House

If you're interested in Grand Canyon's native history, it's definitely worth a visit to Hopi House, which pays homage to the region's tribes. The building was inspired by the architecture at Old Oraibi, a Hopi Village 80 miles east of Grand Canyon that is the oldest continuously inhabited town in the U.S. Designed by famed architect Mary Colter (p.167), Hopi House's stone exterior, thatched ceilings and mud plastered interior walls are all characteristic of traditional Hopi architecture. (Colter did, however, forgo the traditional roof entrance in favor of a front door.) Hopi craftsmen performed much of the construction and masonry, and when the building first opened in 1905 native artisans lived on its upper floors. Native arts and crafts were sold inside, and Hopi songs and dances were performed outside.

The location of Hopi House, directly across from the upscale El Tovar Hotel, was carefully chosen by the buildings' owner, the Fred Harvey Company. At the time, the company was actively promoting Grand Canyon as a tourist destination, and Hopi House offered tourists an intriguing glimpse of the Southwest's exotic native cultures—just a few steps away from their luxury hotel.

Today Hopi House continues its century-old tradition of selling high-quality native crafts. Inside you'll find Navajo blankets, Hopi Kachina dolls, Zuni pottery, and native jewelry from across the Southwest. On weekends, traditional Hopi Dancers often perform outside. If you happen to visit when a Hopi dance is offered, don't pass up a chance to witness this fascinating cultural display.

7 El Tovar Hotel

This historic hotel—the "Ritz of the Divine Abyss"—offers the finest lodging in Grand Canyon. Over the years, El Tovar has played host to such 20th century luminaries as Theodore Roosevelt and Albert Einstein. Even if you're not a guest, El Tovar's dramatic front lobby is worth a quick look, and its bar and restaurant offer the best food and drinks on the South Rim.

When El Tovar first opened in 1905, it was one of the most technologically advanced hotels in the Southwest. Among its high-tech amenities: electric lights, steam heat, indoor plumbing, and hot water—a stark contrast to the primitive rooms, cheap beds, and outhouses that had previously defined luxury at Grand Canyon. For many years, fresh fruits and vegetables were grown in El Tovar's greenhouses, and local farm animals provided fresh eggs and milk. El Tovar was the brainchild of the Santa Fe Railway, which wanted a grand hotel to accommodate the flood of tourists arriving by train. Its architect, Charles Whittlescy, was inspired by the grand chalets of Switzerland.

El Tovar was named after Don Pedro de Tovar, a lieutenant of Spanish explorer Francisco Vásquez de Coronado, who led the first Spanish expedition through the Southwest in 1540. Ironically, Don Pedro de Tovar never set eyes on Grand Canyon. Coronado sent another of his men, García Lopez de Cárdenas, to explore Grand Canyon. When the Fred Harvey Company decided to build the hotel, however, they already had a Cárdenas Hotel in Colorado, so they went with the name El Tovar instead.

View in front of El Tovar

Isis Temple

The Battleship

This long prominent rock formation, named for its physical resemblance to a battleship, is home to a cave used by nesting California condors (p.46).

North Rim (p.253)

Bright Angel Canyon
Slicing eight miles into the North Rim, this dramatic side canyon is home to the North Kaibab Trail (p.274)

Plateau Point (p.175)

Indian Garden
Easily distinguished by its green canopy of cottonwood trees, this lush oasis was once used as a garden by local Indians. Today it's home to a campground used by backpackers on the Bright Angel Trail.

Bright Angel Trail (p.168)

8 Bright Angel Lodge

Perched along a particularly dramatic section of the rim, Bright Angel Lodge is definitely worth a quick glimpse. Inside you'll find a small museum with historic photos and a fireplace built out of actual Grand Canyon rocks—arranged floor to ceiling in their proper geological sequence. A small booth to the left of the front desk also offers information on ranger programs, bus tours, mule rides, and other daily South Rim activities.

The original Bright Angel Hotel offered the first overnight accommodations in Grand Canyon Village. When it opened in 1896, guests could stay at the hotel or in an adjacent tent camp. Guests walked from the tent camp to the hotel along an elevated boardwalk that protected them from mud and horse droppings (a prominent feature of Grand Canyon Village back then). Over the years, the lodge expanded to include a log cabin with eight guest rooms. Cabin rooms were rented for $2.50 per night, and tents were rented for $1.50. The current buildings were designed by Mary Colter in the 1930s.

Geological Fireplace

9 Santa Fe Train Depot

This rustic train station, located just south of El Tovar Hotel, is the only train station in any U.S. national park. It also claims to be the last surviving train station in America built entirely out of logs.

Train service first arrived at the South Rim in 1901, following the completion of a spur line connecting the South Rim to the town of Williams (60 miles to the south). Before the spur line was completed, the most dependable form of transportation to the South Rim was a bumpy, all-day stagecoach ride that coast $20. When the spur line was completed, visitors could travel to the South Rim in four hours for $3.50. Not surprisingly, the railroad brought a flood of new visitors to Grand Canyon. Within a few decades, however, most people were arriving by car, and in 1968 falling ridership forced the railroad to shut down. The last departing train carried only three passengers. Then, in 1989, the railroad roared back to life. With traffic and congestion increasing in the park, a new generation of riders rediscovered the railroad's convenience and charm. Today trains depart daily from Williams.

10 Lookout Studio

This small stone building, perched on the edge of the Canyon just west of Bright Angel Lodge, offers stunning views and an information desk inside. Lookout Studio was designed by Mary Colter, who wanted the building to blend seamlessly into the landscape. This followed the design principles set forth by landscape architect Frederick Law Olmstead, who believed that, whenever possible, buildings in national parks should reflect the architecture of indigenous cultures. The indigenous cultures of the Southwest built some of the most impressive structures in America, and Colter incorporated many of their architectural techniques—stone walls, flat roofs, timber supports—into her design. After it was built, Lookout Studio became famous for its sweeping views. An old Santa Fe Railroad brochure once boasted that visitors who peered through the telescopes installed at Lookout Studio could "traverse the Canyon trails, explore the rugged portions of the interior, or see its faraway reaches."

Lookout Studio, 1915

⑪ Kolb Studio

Today Kolb Studio houses a well-stocked bookstore and art gallery with changing exhibits. But for over 70 years, it was the home of Emery Kolb, one of Grand Canyon's earliest and most famous photographers. Emery and his brother Ellsworth came to Grand Canyon in 1902. Shortly after their arrival, they set up a photography studio on the rim and started hawking souvenir photos of mule riders descending the nearby Bright Angel Trail. But as *Saturday Evening Post* writer Irvin S. Cobb wrote of one such mule ride, "Just under the first terrace a halt is made while the official photographer takes a picture; and when you get back he has your finished copy ready for you, so you can see for yourself just how pale and haggard and wall-eyed and how much like a typhoid patient you looked."

Tourist photos paid the bills, but the Kolb brothers' passion was exploring Grand Canyon and capturing their daredevil exploits on film. In 1911 the brothers ran the Colorado River from Wyoming to California—the first time anyone had accomplished the feat since John Wesley Powell in 1869. But the Kolbs' journey wasn't just for the record books. The brothers filmed their journey and made the first-ever movie of a river trip through Grand Canyon. The Kolbs screened their movie at lectures across the country, and it played continuously at Kolb Studio until Emery's death in 1976.

Emery Kolb

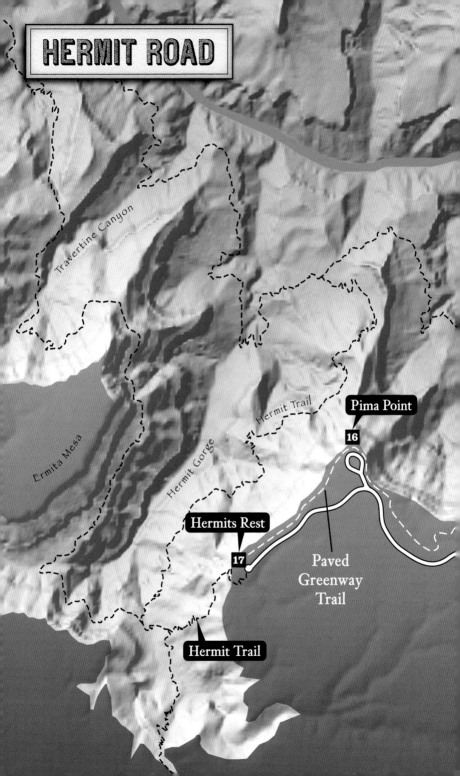

HERMIT ROAD

Travertine Canyon

Ermita Mesa

Hermit Trail

Hermit Gorge

Pima Point

16

Hermits Rest

17

Paved
Greenway
Trail

Hermit Trail

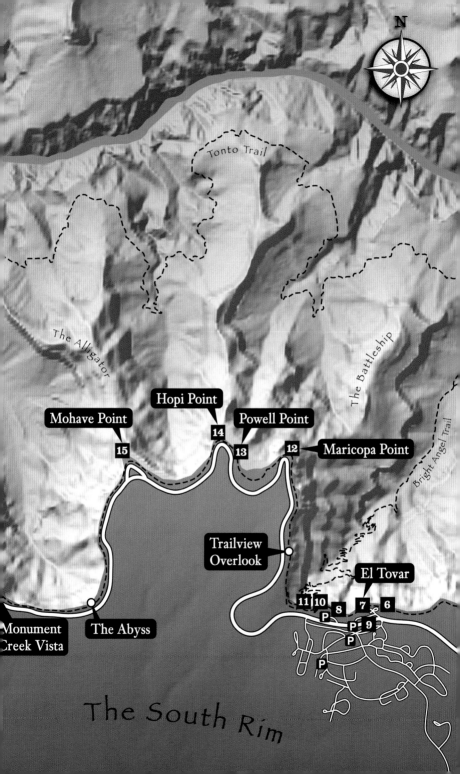

12 Maricopa Point

Maricopa Point offers Hermit Road's first sweeping views of western Grand Canyon. Just west of the point are the remains of the Orphan Mine, one of the most productive uranium mines in America in the 1950s. Prior to the 1950s, the mine site was home to a 20-cabin resort owned by Will Rogers, Jr.

IMAGINE, IF YOU can, a monster of a hollow hundreds of miles long and a mile deep, and anywhere from ten to sixteen miles wide, with a mountain range—the most wonderful mountain range in the world—planted in it . . . Imagine all this spread out beneath the unflawed turquoise of the Arizona sky and washed in the liquid gold of the Arizona sunshine—and if you imagine hard enough and keep it up long enough you may begin, in the course of eight or ten years, to have a faint, a very faint and shadowy conception of this spot where the shamed scheme of creation is turned upside down and the very womb of the world is laid bare before our imperious eyes. Then go to Arizona and see it all for yourself, and you will realize what an entirely inadequate and deficient thing the human imagination is.

—Irvin S. Cobb, 1913

ORPHAN MINE

This former mine, located between Maricopa Point and Powell Point, was one of the country's most productive uranium mines in the 1950s and 60s. The Orphan Mine claim patent was originally filed in 1906 by Dan Hogan, and it was signed by Hogan's old Commandant in the Spanish American War: President Teddy Roosevelt. Copper and other metals were extracted from the Orphan Mine in the early 1900s, and in 1951 high-grade uranium was discovered roughly 1,500 feet below the surface. Although the land around the mine was federally protected from mining activities, the mine itself was considered a private inholding established prior to the creation of the national park. In 1956 a private company began uranium mining operations. Several years later, rich ore veins were discovered that extended beyond the mine's original boundaries, and the company strong-armed the government into expanding the mine's boundaries by threatening to build a 600-room, 18-story hotel on the site. In 1962 President John F. Kennedy signed a law that expanded mining operations near the Orphan Mine in exchange for the title to the claims within 25 years.

The Orphan Mine closed for good in 1969, by which point over 4.2 million pounds of uranium had been extracted. (It has been estimated that Northern Arizona contains roughly 326 million pounds of uranium—the energy equivalent of 11.6 billion barrels of oil.) In 1987 the National Park Service obtained the title to the Orphan Mine. Today the Rim Trail detours around the mine due to concerns of lingering radiation.

🔟 Powell Point

Powell Point is named for John Wesley Powell, a famous explorer who led the first Colorado River expedition through Grand Canyon in 1869. In 1920 a monument to Powell was built and dedicated here. The ceremony was attended by Powell's niece and grand-niece, and the monument was christened by the Secretary of the Interior with water from the Colorado River.

Powell's Grand Canyon adventure has been called the last great expedition of the American West. Prior to the trip, no one knew what existed along much of the Colorado River. There were rumors of giant waterfalls at the bottom of Grand Canyon and places where the river disappeared underground. Accepting these risks, Powell, a one-armed Civil War veteran, and nine other men, none with any whitewater experience, launched four boats from Green River, Wyoming, in May 1869. Three months later, two boats carrying six skeletal men emerged from Grand Canyon near present-day Lake Mead. Four men had abandoned the grueling journey along the way, three of whom died trying to reach civilization. The names of those four men do not appear on the monument. See page 73 for more on John Wesley Powell's extraordinary journey.

14 Hopi Point

Named in honor of the Hopi Indians, Hopi Point offers some of Hermit Road's most sweeping views. Because it juts out farther into the Canyon than any other accessible viewpoint on the South Rim, Hopi Point is one of Grand Canyon's most popular sunset destinations. It also offers terrific views of several stone "temples" rising from the depths of the Canyon. Almost directly ahead lies flat-topped Shiva Temple (named for the Hindu destroyer), and just east of Shiva is pointy Isis Temple (named for the Egyptian goddess of nature). Cheops Pyramid (named for the Great Pyramid of Cheops) lies below Isis to the east. To the northeast, Hopi Point offers dramatic views of Zoroaster Temple.

AT LENGTH, AS the sun draws near the horizon, the great drama of the day begins...Slowly the myriad of details have come out and the walls are flecked with lines of minute tracery...Stronger and sharper becomes the relief of each projection...A thousand forms, hitherto unseen or obscure, start up within the abyss, and stand forth in strength and animation. All things seem to grow in beauty, power, and dimensions. What was grand before has become majestic, the majestic becomes sublime, and, ever expanding and developing, the sublime passes beyond the reach of our faculties and becomes transcendent.

—Clarence Dutton, 1882

ZOROASTER TEMPLE

Zoroaster Temple, visible to the east from Hopi Point, is one of Grand Canyon's most graceful rock formations. The temple is named after the Persian prophet Zoroaster, who founded Zoroastrianism several centuries before Christ. Rising 4,500 feet above the Colorado River (7,128 feet above sea level), Zoroaster Temple is a magnet for ambitious rock climbers. The first ascent of "Zoro" was made on September 23, 1958 by David Ganci and Rick Tidrick. The pair started from Phantom Ranch and spent four days trekking to the top.

15 Mohave Point

Mohave Point is named in honor of the Mojave Indians, who once lived along the lower Colorado River south of Grand Canyon. (And that's not a typo you just saw—as a general rule, "Mojave" is spelled with a "j" for locations in California and with an "h" for locations in Arizona.) The long, rocky promontory that stretches down from Mohave Point is called the Alligator. Hermit Rapid, on the Colorado River, is also visible from Mohave Point. The rapid, like many rapids in Grand Canyon, formed when debris washed into the river from an adjacent side canyon.

IMAGINE, WAY DOWN there at the bottom, a stream visible only at certain favored points because of the mighty intervening ribs and chines of rock—a stream that appears to you as a torpidly crawling yellow worm, its wrinkling back spangled with tarnished white specks, but which is really a wide, deep, brawling, rushing river—the Colorado—full of torrents and rapids; and those white specks you see are the tops of enormous rocks in its bed.

—Irvin S. Cobb, 1913

The Abyss

This appropriately named viewpoint showcases one of Hermit Road's most dramatic sections. From the Canyon's edge, sheer cliffs plunge nearly 3,000 feet. The next shuttle stop to the west, Monument Creek Vista, also offers impressive views of the terrifying drop-offs. Both viewpoints offer a terrific glimpse of Grand Canyon's top six rock layers (p.28), which represent 80 million years of earth history.

16 Pima Point

Pima Point, named after the Pima Indians of southern Arizona, offers one of the best views of the Colorado River along Hermit Road. Although the Pima Indians refer to themselves as *Akimel O'odham* ("River People"), the name Pima is derived from *pim'ach*, which means "I don't understand you." This was probably the unfortunate response given to early Spanish explorers when they asked the *Akimel O'odham* what they called themselves.

In 1912 the Fred Harvey Company built an upscale cluster of tent cabins called Hermit Camp 3,600 feet below Pima Point. Hermit Camp was located along the Hermit Trail—the Santa Fe Railroad's free alternative to the Bright Angel Trail, which was then operated as a private toll road. Hermit Camp boasted such amenities as showers, telephones, a dining hall, a stable, and a blacksmith's shop. Guests often stayed for several days, spending their time exploring the rugged surroundings on foot or horseback.

In 1926 a 6,300-foot aerial tram was built connecting Pima Point and Hermit Camp. At the time it was the longest single-span tram in the United States, and the ride was about 30 minutes each way. In the late 1920s, however, the park gained control of the Bright Angel Trail and lifted its $1 per person toll. Before long, most Grand Canyon visitors were descending the Canyon via the Bright Angel Trail, which is closer to the park's hotels, and in 1930 Hermit Camp shut down for good. Its remains were burned and the tram was removed. Today the remains of Hermit Camp are faintly visible below.

17 Hermits Rest

Hermits Rest marks the end of Hermit Road. Its main attraction is a whimsical stone building with a giant fireplace. Drinks, snacks, and gifts are available inside, and restrooms are located nearby. Hermits Rest was built by the Santa Fe Railroad in 1914. Like many famous buildings in the park, it was designed by architect Mary Colter, who wanted to create a building that looked like the kind of place where a hermit might live. In addition to the main building, she also designed a limestone arch with an authentic mission bell from New Mexico.

The "hermit" of Hermits Rest was an early prospector named Louis Boucher, who lived by himself in the canyon below. Although labeled a hermit, Boucher was, by all accounts, a friendly man who simply liked living alone. Originally from Quebec, Boucher arrived at Grand Canyon around 1891. Like many prospectors, he had several horses and mules. Unlike many prospectors, he kept goldfish in a small trough. Boucher also planted an orchard that provided him with peaches, oranges and figs. After spending two decades searching in vain for a rich mineral strike, Boucher left Grand Canyon and moved to Utah.

Louis Boucher

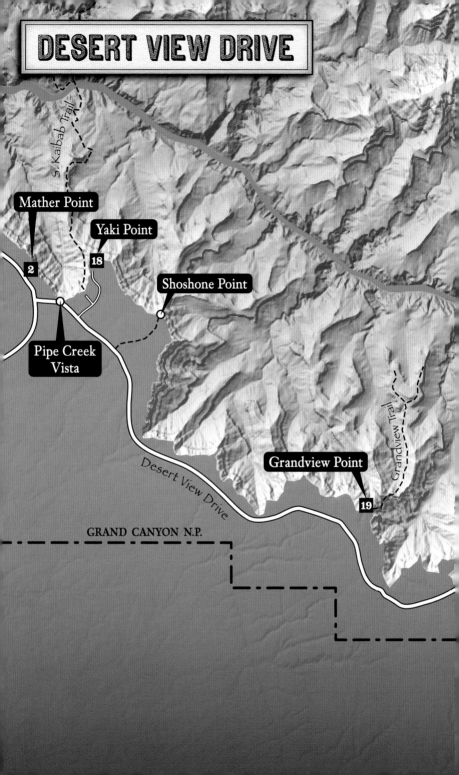

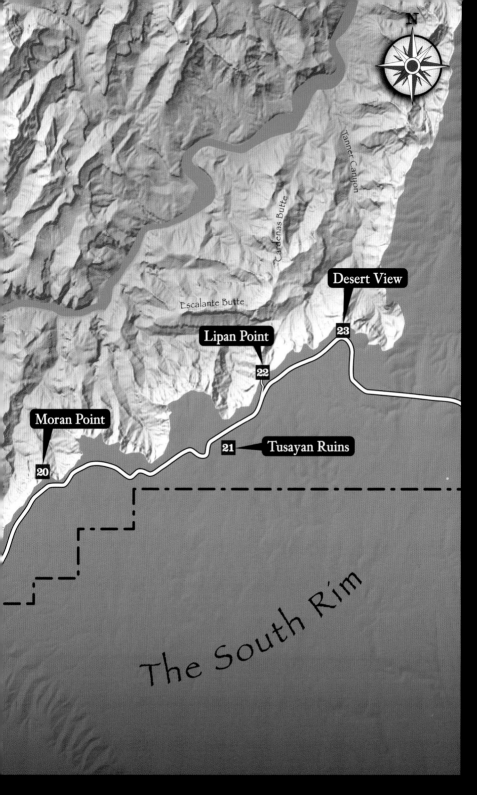

Pipe Creek Vista

This dramatic viewpoint, located just before the turnoff to Yaki Point, offers impressive views of O'Neil Butte (below).

18 Yaki Point

Stretching far into the Canyon, Yaki Point provides sweeping views to the east and west, making it one of the best sunrise spots on the South Rim. From March through November, the road to Yaki Point is only accessible via the park's free shuttle (check *The Guide* for schedules). The South Kaibab Trail (p.178), which offers the South Rim's most direct route to the bottom of the Canyon, starts just south of Yaki Point. You can see the trail as it cuts diagonally across the east face of O'Neil Butte (above). Yaki Point was supposedly named by George Wharton James in honor of Mexico's Yaqui Indians, who were victims of mass genocide in the early 1900s.

IMAGINE—IF IT be winter—snowdrifts above, with desert flowers blooming alongside the drifts, and down below great stretches of green verdure; imagine two or three separate snowstorms visibly raging at different points, with clear, bright stretches of distance intervening between them, and nearer maybe a splendid rainbow arching downward into the great void; for these meteorological three-ring circuses are not uncommon at certain seasons.

—Irvin S. Cobb, 1913

Shoshone Point

This sweeping viewpoint offers some of the South Rim's most incredible scenery, but because reaching it requires a one-mile stroll along an unmarked trail, remarkably few people ever visit. The "hike" (elevation change: 50 feet) to Shoshone Point follows a dirt access road 1.3 miles east of the Yaki Point turnoff (6.3 miles west of Grandview Point). The "trailhead" is a locked metal gate that's easy to walk around. (Don't worry, hiking along the road is 100% OK unless Shoshone point has been reserved for a wedding or other private event.) After a roughly 20-minute stroll, you'll come to a group picnic area with tables, grills and an outhouse. Shoshone Point is located at the end of the prominent rock ledge nearby.

VISHNU TEMPLE

Rising to a maximum height of 7,533 feet, the pyramidal spire of Vishnu Temple is easily recognizable from many viewpoints along Desert View Drive. Like many prominent landmarks in Grand Canyon, Vishnu Temple was named by the geologist Clarence Dutton in the late 1870s. Dutton felt that many Grand Canyon landmarks bore a striking resemblance to the ancient temples of the Orient, and he named them accordingly. Vishnu Temple is named for Vishnu, the four-armed Supreme Being of Hinduism.

19 Grandview Point

At 7,406 feet, Grandview Point is one of the highest points on the South Rim. It is also the jumping off point for the popular Grandview Trail (p.190).

Before the first railroad arrived at Grand Canyon Village in 1901, Grandview Point was the hub of all tourist activity in the park. In 1886 John Hance (p.76) built Grand Canyon's first hotel here, and within a few years a prospector named Pete Berry built the Grandview Hotel (above). When the railroad arrived in Grand Canyon Village, however, few tourists were willing to make the additional trek to Grandview Point, and by 1908 both hotels had shut down. A few years later, Berry sold his landholdings to newspaper tycoon William Randolph Hearst, who tore down the Grandview Hotel in 1929. Hearst planned to build his own hotel on the property, but a federal court forced him to sell his land to the park in 1939.

During its short-lived hotel era, Grandview Point was a popular jumping off point for miners seeking riches below the rim. In the early 1890s Pete Berry helped establish the Grandview Mine, and the Grandview Trail was built to haul copper ore out of the Canyon. The Grandview Mine contained an extremely high-grade ore (up to 70 percent copper), but when copper prices crashed in 1907 the mine shut down. Then, in 1971, a mineralogist conducting research at Grandview Mine discovered a beautiful turquoise mineral (right), which was officially classified as the new mineral species "Grandviewite" in 2007.

Moran Point

20 Moran Point

This impressive overlook is named after Thomas Moran, one of America's most famous and influential landscape painters. Born in England in 1837, Moran moved to America with his family in the mid-1800s, a time when landscape painting exhibitions drew blockbuster crowds in Eastern cities. In the days before color photography, monumental landscape paintings offered the public a rare glimpse of America's wild and exotic places. Inspired by these works, young Thomas Moran decided to become a landscape painter, and his dramatic paintings of Yellowstone were critical in the establishment of Yellowstone National Park in 1872. The following year, Moran joined legendary explorer John Wesley Powell on an expedition to Grand Canyon. He later wrote of his experience, "it was by far the most awfully grand and impressive scene that I have ever yet seen." Moran later returned with geologist Clarence Dutton, and his works from both of these trips were published in best-selling books. One of his paintings, *The Grand Chasm of the Colorado*, hung in the U.S. Capitol for many years. Deeply moved by his Grand Canyon experiences, Moran returned to the Canyon every winter for over 20 years.

21 Tusayan Ruin

These stone ruins mark the location of Tusayan, a small Ancestral Puebloan ("Anasazi") village that existed here 800 years ago. The remains were partially excavated in 1930, and today they are the most impressive archaeological ruins on the South Rim. A short paved path guides visitors through the ruins, but the best way to experience Tusayan is to join one of the free ranger-guided tours offered throughout the day. Also be sure to check out the nearby museum, which is filled with fascinating artifacts.

At its peak, the village of Tusayan was probably home to no more than about 30 people, and archaeologists believe it was only occupied for about 25 years between A.D. 1185 and A.D. 1210. Tusayan was one of the last Ancestral Puebloan sites occupied in Grand Canyon. It was constructed shortly before the total collapse of Ancestral Puebloan society (p.59). The most prominent feature of the village was a large 14-room building with two *kivas* (ceremonial rooms) located nearby. The structures offered good views of the San Francisco Peaks, which the Hopi, who are descended from the Ancestral Puebloans, believe are home to natural spirits called *katsinas* (p.60).

The residents of Tusayan hunted wild game, gathered wild plants, and cultivated beans, corn and squash in a field to the east. Because there is no permanent water source within seven miles of the village, stone walls were built in the fields to retain runoff from rainstorms. The water was then stored in clay pots and woven baskets waterproofed with piñon pine pitch.

22 Lipan Point

Lipan Point offers one of the most sweeping views on the South Rim. It's also one of the best places to catch a rare glimpse of rocks belonging to the Grand Canyon Supergroup, which are absent from much of the Canyon. These rocks range in age from 800 million to 1.2 billion years old, making them some of the oldest rocks in Grand Canyon. They are easily visible above the sharp bend in the Colorado River across from Lipan Point. (Look for the colorful rock layers tilted at an obvious 20-degree angle.) As you stare out at the rock layers of the Grand Canyon Supergroup, ponder just how old they really are. Back when these rocks formed, plants and land animals had not yet evolved, and Earth's continents were barren rocks, more similar to Mars than the landscapes we know today.

Below the rocks of the Grand Canyon Supergroup, the Colorado River twists and turns in a prominent, S-shaped bend. The broad, circular delta that forms the bend is called Unkar Delta, and it played an important role in Grand Canyon's human prehistory. Roughly 1,000 years ago, Unkar Delta was home to a farming community of Ancestral Puebloans (p.59). Archaeologists believe that as many as ten families lived here. They built small stone houses and grew corn, beans and squash on the fertile delta. In the summer, when Unkar Delta became scorching hot, they climbed to the North Rim and farmed dozens of sites on its broad, flat plateaus. After harvesting those crops, they returned to the depths of the Canyon. Unkar Delta was inhabited for roughly 300 years, and today it contains the largest complex of archaeological sites along the Colorado River.

23 Desert View

Desert View is the final stop on Desert View Drive. At 7,438 feet, it's one of the highest points on the South Rim, and it offers one of the South Rim's most spectacular views. At most viewpoints, the Colorado River is not visible at all or appears as a tiny speck. Desert View reveals the Colorado River in its full glory as it emerges from narrow Marble Canyon (p.216) and begins its journey west into the heart of Grand Canyon. Notice the deep gorge that slices into the broad plateau to the east, just upstream of the visible portion of the river. This gorge was cut by the Little Colorado River, the Colorado River's largest tributary in Grand Canyon. The broad, flat plateau beyond the Little Colorado River belongs to the Navajo Indian Reservation.

Desert View is famous for Desert View Watchtower, a 70-foot stone tower built in 1932. Designed by Mary Colter (p.167), the watchtower was inspired by ancient stone towers in the Four Corners region. A circular staircase ascends the tower, the interior of which is decorated with reproductions of Ancestral Puebloan petroglyphs and depictions of Hopi legends. The top of the tower is the highest point on the South Rim (7,522 feet), and large windows offer spectacular 360-degree views of the surrounding landscape.

Desert View is also home to the Desert View Visitor Center and Bookstore. There's also a small snack bar nearby, as well as a gas station and the Desert View Campground. Continue along Desert View Drive and you'll reach the park's East Entrance Station.

Desert View Watchtower

Architect of the Southwest
MARY COLTER

In the early 1900s, a time when few women practiced architecture, Mary Colter was hard at work designing some of the most spectacular buildings in Arizona. Her creations, several of which are found in Grand Canyon, helped define an aesthetic that successfully complemented the grand natural landscapes of the American Southwest.

As a young girl growing up in St. Paul, Minnesota, Mary Jane Colter was captivated by the artwork of the local Sioux Indians. She later studied art in San Francisco, and in 1901 she was hired by the Fred Harvey Company to decorate the interior of an Indian craft giftshop in Albuquerque. At the time, the Fred Harvey Company operated a successful string of hotels and restaurants along the Santa Fe Railway. The company realized, however, that Eastern travelers were fascinated by the indigenous people of the Southwest—and eager to buy their beautiful baskets and rugs. Following the success of the Albuquerque giftshop, the company decided to build another Indian craft giftshop next to the opulent El Tovar hotel in Grand Canyon. Mary Colter was selected as the architect given her talent and interest with native design.

The design of Hopi House, as the building came to be called, was a striking contrast to El Tovar. Whereas El Tovar was inspired by Swiss chalets, Hopi House was inspired by Old Oraibi, an 800-year-old pueblo. Rather than look down upon indigenous designs in deference to classical European styles, Colter immersed herself in the minutia of native architecture. She diligently studied Hopi designs to faithfully replicate them, and during construction she insisted on working with local materials so that the building blended seamlessly with the environment. Her goal was to create a structure that complemented the beautiful landscape, rather than structures that competed with it.

Hopi House opened to wide acclaim, and Colter went on to design some of Grand Canyon's most famous buildings: Lookout Studio, Hermits Rest, Phantom Ranch, Desert View Watchtower, and Bright Angel Lodge. A woman of strong will and boundless energy, Colter ruffled many feathers while working on her projects. She was a perfectionist who often drove workmen crazy in her quest to create perfectly imperfect designs. As she once remarked about Hermits Rest, "You can't imagine what it cost to make it look this old." Although Colter's designs are often romanticized, her rejection of classical European traditions in favor of indigenous styles was a revelation at the time. Today her buildings are among the most popular and timeless in Grand Canyon.

❧ BRIGHT ANGEL TRAIL ❧

SUMMARY The Bright Angel Trail is the most popular trail on the South Rim—and with good reason. Starting near several popular hotels, it provides convenient access below the rim, offering dramatic views of the Inner Canyon. Although steep and challenging, it's well-maintained and makes a terrific introduction to Inner Canyon hiking. Day hikers should consider 1.5 Mile Resthouse (2–4 hours, round-trip) or 3 Mile Resthouse (4–6 hours, round-trip). Both offer clean drinking water in the summer months. Halfway down the trail is Indian Garden Campground, and a nearby spur trail heads 1.5 miles to Plateau Point, one of the finest Inner Canyon viewpoints in the park. Past Indian Garden, the Bright Angel Trail continues its steep descent to the Colorado River, plunging 200 feet through Vishnu Schist along Devils Corkscrew, a dramatic series of switchbacks. The trail ends at the Bright Angel Suspension Bridge, which continues across the Colorado River to Bright Angel Campground and Phantom Ranch.

TRAILHEAD The Bright Angel Trail starts next to Kolb's Studio, just west of the Bright Angel Lodge.

TRAIL INFO

RATING: Strenuous

HIKING TIME: 2–3 Days

DISTANCE: 15.6 miles, round-trip

ELEVATION CHANGE: 4,285 ft.

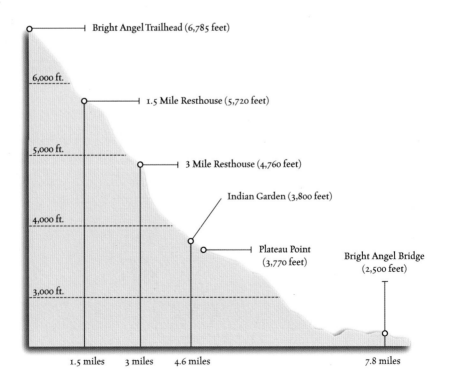

Bright Angel Trailhead (6,785 feet)

6,000 ft.

1.5 Mile Resthouse (5,720 feet)

5,000 ft.

3 Mile Resthouse (4,760 feet)

Indian Garden (3,800 feet)

4,000 ft.

Plateau Point
(3,770 feet)

Bright Angel Bridge
(2,500 feet)

3,000 ft.

1.5 miles   3 miles   4.6 miles   7.8 miles

Devils Corkscrew, Bright Angel Trail

PLATEAU POINT is one of the Inner Canyon's most stunning destinations. Perched 1,300 feet above the Colorado River, it treats hikers and mule riders to sweeping 360-degree views of some of the Canyon's most famous landmarks. If you're spending the night in Indian Garden Campground on the Bright Angel Trail, Plateau Point makes a fantastic sunrise or sunset destination. The 1.5-mile trail to Plateau Point is reached via the Tonto Trail near Indian Garden Campground. After crossing Garden Creek just below Indian Garden, follow the Tonto Trail west for roughly three quarters of a mile until reaching a fork; turn right and walk across the broad, flat platform to Plateau Point.

PHANTOM RANCH

Nestled in a narrow canyon not far from the Colorado River, Phantom Ranch offers Grand Canyon's only overnight lodging below the rim. Eleven rustic cabins and two dormitories are scattered along the banks of Bright Angel Creek and shaded by towering cottonwood trees. A central dining hall serves home-cooked meals to guests, and showers and flush toilets add a touch of backcountry luxury. An overnight stay at Phantom Ranch is, without question, one of the highlights of Grand Canyon National Park. There are three ways to get to Phantom Ranch: by mule, on foot, or by raft. Overnight mule rides ($507) start from the South Rim and head down the Bright Angel Trail. Overnight reservations for hikers are much harder to come by due to the bargain price ($46 dorm room, $150 private cabin). Although reservations (888-297-2757) are accepted up to 13 months in advance, most spaces sell out within a few hours on the first day of availability. Finally, some rafting trips drop passengers off at Phantom Ranch, where they spend the night before hiking out the next day.

⊸ SOUTH KAIBAB TRAIL ᔕ

SUMMARY   Steep and strenuous, the South Kaibab Trail is the South Rim's most direct route to the bottom of the Canyon. While most Inner Canyon trails follow side canyons, the South Kaibab Trail follows open ridgelines, providing spectacular views in all directions, which is great for day hikers. If you're day hiking, consider the 1.5-mile hike to Ooh-Aah Point (2–4 hours, round-trip). The South Kaibab Trail ends at the Kaibab Suspension Bridge, which heads to Bright Angel Campground and Phantom Ranch. (If you're planning an overnight backpack to Bright Angel Campground or Phantom Ranch, consider hiking down the South Kaibab Trail and returning via the Bright Angel Trail, which is longer but slightly more gradual.) Note: There's no water on the South Kaibab Trail.

TRAILHEAD   The trail starts near Yaki Point (p.150), but private vehicles are not allowed at the trailhead. Free shuttles head to the South Kaibab Trailhead throughout the day from Canyon View Information Plaza. In the early morning, another shuttle departs from Bright Angel Lodge and the Backcountry Information Center. Check *The Guide* for seasonal schedules.

◗ TRAIL INFO ◖

RATING: Strenuous	**HIKING TIME:** 2 Days
DISTANCE: 14.6 miles, round-trip	**ELEVATION CHANGE:** 4,700 ft.

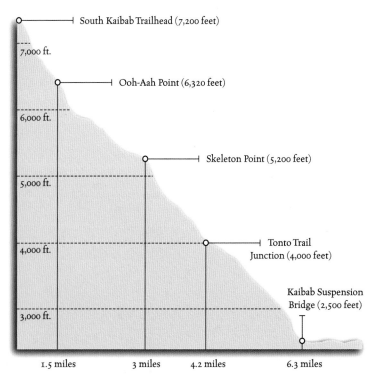

South Kaibab Trailhead (7,200 feet)

7,000 ft.

Ooh-Aah Point (6,320 feet)

6,000 ft.

Skeleton Point (5,200 feet)

5,000 ft.

Tonto Trail
Junction (4,000 feet)

4,000 ft.

Kaibab Suspension
Bridge (2,500 feet)

3,000 ft.

1.5 miles   3 miles   4.2 miles   6.3 miles

SOUTH KAIBAB TRAIL

South Kaibab Trail

⊰ HERMIT TRAIL ⊱

SUMMARY Although less famous than the popular Bright Angel Trail, the Hermit trail is one of the South Rim's best hikes. Departing from Hermits Rest, it treats hikers to spectacular western vistas as it descends to the Colorado River in two steep drops. Though unmaintained, the Hermit Trail is generally in good condition with a few tricky but manageable washouts. Day hikers can head 2.5 miles to Santa Maria Spring (5–8 hours, round-trip). The Hermit Trail ends along the banks of the Colorado River next to Hermit Rapid—one of the most thrilling rapids in Grand Canyon. If you're lucky, you'll catch a glimpse of river runners hooting and hollering as they barrel through the waves. Backpackers must camp at designated campsites at either Hermit Creek Campsite (located just west of the Hermit Trail along the Tonto Trail) or at Hermit Rapid.

TRAILHEAD The Hermit Trail starts west of Hermits Rest (p.144) at the end of Hermit Road. Overnight hikers can park at the trailhead (you'll be given a code to open the gate to Hermit Road); day hikers can ride the free shuttle to Hermits Rest.

◆ TRAIL INFO ◆

RATING: Strenuous	**HIKING TIME:** 2–3 Days
DISTANCE: 18.6 miles, round-trip	**ELEVATION CHANGE:** 4,240 ft.

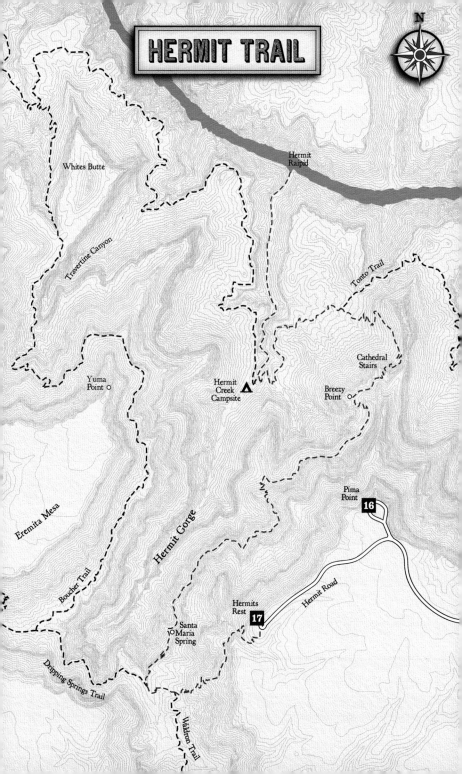

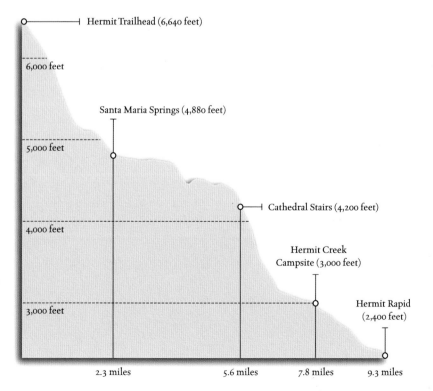

Hermit Trailhead (6,640 feet)

6,000 feet

Santa Maria Springs (4,880 feet)

5,000 feet

Cathedral Stairs (4,200 feet)

4,000 feet

Hermit Creek
Campsite (3,000 feet)

Hermit Rapid
(2,400 feet)

3,000 feet

2.3 miles   5.6 miles   7.8 miles   9.3 miles

HERMIT TRAIL

Hermit Trail

ᐱ GRANDVIEW TRAIL ᕫ

SUMMARY   The steep Grandview Trail, which drops roughly 2,600 feet from Grandview Point to Grandview Mesa, is one of the few Inner Canyon trails that doesn't descend all the way to the Colorado River. Mellow day hikers can enjoy the outstanding views along the first quarter mile of the trail. Energetic day hikers can head all the way to the campground at Horseshoe Mesa (6–9 hours, round-trip). There are no water sources on Horseshoe Mesa, so backpackers must bring their own water for drinking and cooking. Several trails descend roughly 1,000 feet from Horseshoe Mesa to the Tonto Trail. If you're spending the night, a brief hike to the stunning overlook at the eastern tip of Horseshoe Mesa makes a great day trip. Note: There are many abandoned copper mines in the vicinity of Horseshoe Mesa. Do not enter abandoned mines, which can be extremely danger-ous due to steep drop-offs and toxic gases.

TRAILHEAD   The Grandview Trail starts at Grandview Point (p.157), about 12 miles east of Grand Canyon Village on Desert View Drive. There is a parking area next to the trailhead.

◆ TRAIL INFO ◆

RATING: Strenuous

DISTANCE: 6 miles, round-trip

HIKING TIME: 1–2 Days

ELEVATION CHANGE: 2,500 ft.

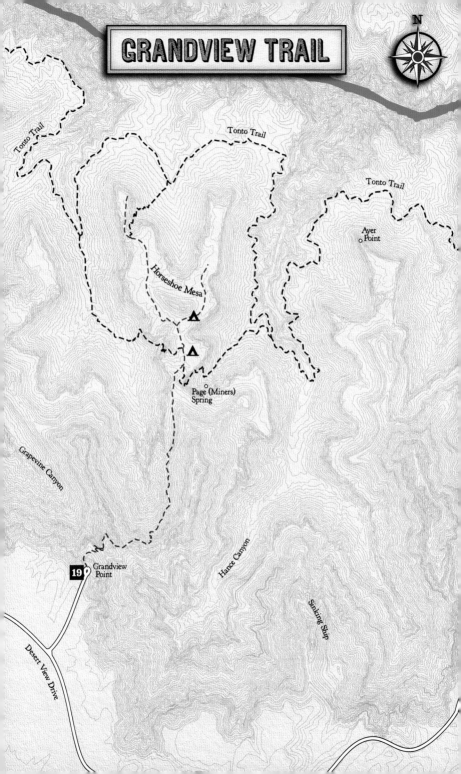

GRANDVIEW TRAIL

N

Tonto Trail

Tonto Trail

Tonto Trail

Ayer
Point

Horseshoe Mesa

△

△

Page (Miners)
Spring

Grapevine Canyon

19 Grandview
Point

Hance Canyon

Sinking Ship

Desert View Drive

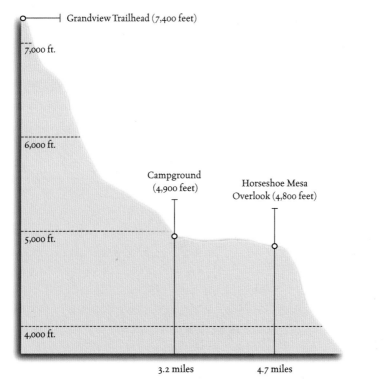

Grandview Trailhead (7,400 feet)

7,000 ft.

6,000 ft.

Campground
(4,900 feet)

Horseshoe Mesa
Overlook (4,800 feet)

5,000 ft.

4,000 ft.

3.2 miles

4.7 miles

THE COLORADO RIVER

✮ ✮ ✮ ✮ ✮

COLORADO RIVER

THE COLORADO RIVER is the heart and soul of Grand Canyon. Without it, the Grand Canyon would be just another quiet stretch of land rolling through northern Arizona. Instead, the river has cut a mile into the surrounding landscape, exposed nearly two billion years worth of Earth's history, and flushed out over 1,000 cubic miles of eroded debris. The result is the single most impressive natural feature in North America.

As stunning as the view is from the rim, the view from the river is even more spectacular. Flowing downstream from Lees Ferry (just south of the Utah/Arizona border), the Colorado enters the most scenic stretch of whitewater in America. As the river cascades down a series of thrilling rapids, sheer cliffs rise up thousands of feet on either side. Twisting deep into the heart of the Canyon, the river exposes a dazzling natural world filled with towering rock formations, sandy beaches, dark caverns, and sparkling waterfalls. Side canyons spread out in all directions, channelling unlikely streams through the parched terrain. While the Colorado glides and swirls around sharp bends in the Canyon, cool shadows mingle with shimmering river light.

As the largest river in the Southwest, the Colorado is a river of liquid gold. Its water, delivered via massive aqueducts, allows millions of people to live in the desert and enables farmers to grow billions of dollars of crops year-round. Although plugged by dams and reservoirs along much of its length, the Colorado flows free in Grand Canyon for 277 miles, providing river runners with some of the most spectacular river scenery in America.

Only 20,000 people—less than half of one percent of all park visitors—embark on a river trip through Grand Canyon each year. The number of river runners is limited by the park service to preserve the pristine wilderness at the bottom of the Canyon. Those lucky enough to witness Grand Canyon from the Colorado are filled with an overpowering sense of awe. Physically, the size of Grand Canyon is humbling. Visually, it's one of the most dynamic places in the world, changing with the weather, the seasons, and the particular time of day. Even seasoned world travelers admit that a river trip through Grand Canyon is one of the most remarkable journeys on the planet.

NATURAL HISTORY

FROM START TO finish, the Colorado River passes through some of the most beautiful and varied terrain in North America. Born in the deep gorges of the upper Rocky Mountains, it plunges headfirst down the pine-covered slopes to emerge in the desert Southwest. The river cuts through the wind-swept canyons of Utah, tears deep into the Grand Canyon, and then glides through the California desert. By the time it crosses the Mexican border to empty into the Gulf of California, the river has passed through seven western states and drained an area the size of Iraq.

The Colorado River is often referred to as the "Nile of America." At first glance, this comparison seems appropriate. Both rivers pass through vast desert regions and both sustain vast desert civilizations along the way. But despite these two basic similarities, the rivers share little else in common. In terms of size, the Colorado is a much smaller river, draining a quarter of the land that the Nile drains. In terms of length, the Colorado's 1,400 miles pales in comparison to the Nile's 4,000.

Even in America, the Colorado lacks many impressive statistics. It's not the longest river in America. Six other rivers are longer. Nor is it the biggest river in America. In terms of annual flow, the Colorado doesn't even rank in the top 25. But what the Colorado does have, and what makes it so remarkable, is the wildest and most terrifying elevation drop of any river in North America.

From its headwaters in the Rocky Mountains to the Gulf of California, the Colorado drops over 13,000 vertical feet. This steep drop, occurring over a relatively short distance, churns up a river that is fast and furious, dropping an average of 7.7 feet per mile—25 times steeper than the mighty Mississippi. Because a river's erosive power increases exponentially with its speed, the Colorado would be a highly destructive river in any part of the world. But in the desert Southwest—a crumbling landscape filled with soft rocks and sparse vegetation—its erosive power is monumental.

As the Colorado enters the Southwest, it grinds away at the region's barren rocks, picking up tiny particles of sediment along the way. The more sediment the river picks up, the more abrasive it becomes. The more abrasive it becomes, the more sediment it picks up. This vicious cycle feeds on itself until the Colorado is (quite literally) a river of liquid sandpaper. Before massive dams plugged the Colorado, the river's sediment loads were phenomenal. Back then, the Colorado carried an average of 235,000 tons of sediment through the Grand Canyon *each day*. "Too thick to drink, too thin to plow," was how one early explorer described it. The river's composition was often two parts sediment to one part water, and because the sediment had a high concentration of iron-oxide, the virgin Colorado had a distinct reddish hue.

The virgin Colorado was also psychotically unpredictable. Early explorers often compared it to a bull. It was an "angry bull," a "blooded bull," and a "wild bull of destruction." The Colorado's flows in Grand Canyon varied anywhere between 3,000 and 200,000 cubic feet of water (90 to 6,000 tons) per second, sometimes within a matter of weeks. The largest flows occurred in the spring, when snowmelt from the Rocky Mountains set loose months of accumulated precipitation. In any given year, snowmelt accounts for over 70 percent of the Colorado River's flow.

The Colorado's spring floods were biblical in proportion. Roaring through the Southwest, they ripped out vegetation, eroded huge chunks of the riverbank, and tumbled 20-ton boulders like ice cubes. During these floods, the river carried its heaviest sediment loads, devouring the landscape at an astonishing rate.

But by winter the Colorado would slow to a trickle and hover just above freezing—a stark contrast to summertime highs when the river often topped 80

SEDIMENT LOAD

The amount of sediment a river can carry increases to the sixth power of its speed. A river flowing at 2 mph will carry 64 times more sediment (2^6=64) than a river flowing at 1 mph (1^6=1). Likewise, a river flowing at 10 mph will carry 1 million times more sediment than a river flowing at 1 mph. During spring floods, the virgin Colorado often flowed at speeds topping 40 mph, carrying up to 27 million tons of sediment through Grand Canyon *each day*. During these floods, Grand Canyon experienced its most intense erosion.

degrees. An entire ecosystem evolved to live in these harrowing conditions. The humpback chub, a fish found only in the Colorado, has a lifecycle timed to the river's wild temperature swings. It also has strong muscles and an uncanny sense of fluid dynamics to keep from washing away during spring floods. Plants were also influenced by the flooding. Apache plume, mesquite, and catclaw acacia grew only above the flood zone.

As the Colorado travels to the sea, it passes through an amazing diversity of landscapes. In Grand Canyon alone, the river encounters three of North America's four deserts. Vegetation typical of the Great Basin Desert, found in Nevada and western Utah, is visible from Lees Ferry to river mile 39. At river mile 39, the Colorado enters the northernmost outpost of the Sonoran Desert, covering much of Arizona, Southern California, and northern Mexico. At river mile 157, the Colorado enters the Mojave Desert, the smallest of the four deserts, but home to such national treasures as Death Valley and Joshua Tree National Park.

The Colorado River in Grand Canyon is on average 300 feet wide and 25 feet deep. Within the Canyon, the river is essentially a series of long pools interrupted by short, quick rapids. Although rapids only account for 10 percent of the Colorado's 277-mile length in Grand Canyon, they account for nearly half of its 2,000-foot elevation drop, and the velocity of water in rapids is up to 10 times greater than in the long pools in between. On most rivers, rapids form wherever the riverbed naturally drops. But in Grand Canyon, rapids form next to side canyons where flash floods have dumped debris into the Colorado. The debris constricts the river and backs it up, creating a steep drop-off—the rapid. Some of these rapids, which can drop up to 30 feet in a matter of seconds, are considered among the most thrilling whitewater in North America.

CERTAIN DEATH

In 1849 an Indian who spoke no English attempted to describe the Colorado River to would-be river runner William Manly. Using a stick to draw in the sand, he mapped the upper Colorado passing through mountains, valleys, and canyons. He then piled up stones to represent the deepest canyon of all. According to Manly, the Indian, "stood with one foot on each side of his river and put his hands on the stones and then raised them as high as he could, making a continued e-e-e-e-e as long as his breath would last, pointed to the canoe and made signs with his hands how it would roll and pitch in the rapids and finally capsize and throw us all out. He then made signs of death to show us that it was a fatal place. I understood perfectly from this that below the valley where we now were was a terrible [canyon], much higher than any we had passed, and the rapids were not navigable with safety."

THE NEW COLORADO

TODAY GRAND CANYON is an oasis of uninterrupted whitewater on a river plugged with dams. Below Grand Canyon, Hoover Dam holds back Lake Mead, the largest man-made lake in the Western Hemisphere. Above Grand Canyon, Glen Canyon Dam holds back Lake Powell, the second largest man-made lake in the Western Hemisphere. Almost all of the water that enters Grand Canyon now passes through the turbines at Glen Canyon Dam, a fact that has significantly altered the downstream ecology.

Since the floodgates at Glen Canyon Dam closed in 1963, the Colorado River in Grand Canyon has undergone a dramatic transformation. Its flow, temperature, and sediment load—the defining characteristics of the river—have all changed. Other than the path it follows, the new Colorado bears almost no resemblance to the pre-dam river.

Historically, the amount of water flowing through Grand Canyon was determined by the amount of precipitation that fell on the Colorado River Basin. Today, the amount of water flowing through Grand Canyon is determined by the engineers at Glen Canyon Dam. Maximum flows are capped at less than 10 percent of what they once were, and the massive spring floods that created much of Grand Canyon have been eliminated. This lack of flooding has created several problems. Most notably, much of the debris washed into the river through side canyons now lies dormant on the bottom of the river. Before the dam, spring floods cleared out the debris and washed it downstream.

Although Glen Canyon Dam smoothed out the river's seasonal flows, daily flows became wildly erratic. The amount of water released from the dam is based on the region's fluctuating power demand, and during peak hours in the afternoon, dam operators can charge twice as much for electricity as they can at night. When Glen Canyon Dam first opened, daily flows fluctuated anywhere between 3,000 and 31,500 cubic feet per second. Downstream, the river rose and fell like a toilet bowl. Daily tides often topped 13 feet and beaches along the banks of the river eroded at an unnaturally high rate. In 1992 the Grand Canyon Protection Act was passed, which required dam operators to smooth out releases in an attempt to reduce beach erosion.

Glen Canyon Dam has also affected the Colorado River's sediment load. Ninety percent of the sediment that used to enter Grand Canyon is now trapped behind Glen Canyon Dam, and each year Lake Powell fills up with more and more sediment—a problem that future generations will have to contend with. In the meantime, water drawn from Lake Powell enters Grand Canyon almost completely silt free.

The water released by Glen Canyon Dam is drawn from the chilly depths of Lake Powell, entering Grand Canyon at a constant 45 degrees. Not surprisingly,

DISAPPEARING BEACHES

Before GLEN CANYON Dam was constructed in 1963, the banks of the Colorado in Grand Canyon were lined with hundreds of sandy beaches. Replenished each spring by the virgin Colorado's annual floods, the beaches provided valuable habitat for native species and were used as campsites by early river runners. But following the construction of Glen Canyon Dam, the river's sediment load in Grand Canyon was reduced by 90 percent, and the beaches started to erode. Adding to the problem were the dam's erratic releases, which were timed to coincide with daily fluctuations in power demand. The releases created huge tides that stripped additional sand from the beaches and flushed it out of Grand Canyon.

In 1992 President George H.W. Bush signed the Grand Canyon Protection Act, which ordered Glen Canyon Dam to operate in a way that protected and enhanced Grand Canyon National Park, including smoothing out daily releases. Maximum flows were capped at 26,000 cubic feet per second (cfs), and daily fluctuations were limited to 8,000 cfs.

Scientists were convinced that smoothed-out flows would significantly reduce Grand Canyon beach erosion. But to their dismay, beach erosion continued at a steady rate. It turned out that new sediment deposited by tributary

streams—enough, theoretically, to replenish the beaches—was languishing at the bottom of the river. What Grand Canyon needed, the scientists concluded, was an old-fashioned flood to stir up the sediment and redeposit it on the riverbank.

In March 1996 Secretary of the Interior Bruce Babbitt turned the wheel at Glen Canyon Dam to release a controlled flood of 45,000 cfs. The flood churned up the river and created more than 50 new beaches. Within a year, however, many of those beaches had disappeared. The flood, it turned out, didn't so much create new beaches as wash existing beaches further downstream. Some scientists blamed the failure on the timing of the flood. Most tributary streams deposit new sediment into Grand Canyon during the rainy summer season. But the flood was conducted in the spring when much of the new sediment had already been washed out of the Canyon. In 2004 a second controlled flood was released in November, when the river contained significantly more sediment, and additional floods were released in March 2008, November 2012 and November 2013. The long-term effects of these floods are still being monitored.

In the end, the controlled floods stirred up as much controversy as they did sediment. And as the Southwest continues to grow, each drop of water in Lake Powell becomes more valuable than ever. Many oppose sacrificing this water to test unproven theories, but something needs to be done before Grand Canyon's beaches disappear for good.

this frigid water has significantly altered the Colorado's ecosystem. For millions of years, fish native to the Colorado had their life cycles timed to the river's wild temperature swings. They could survive in the cold winter water, but needed warm summer water to spawn. Now that the warm water has disappeared, Grand Canyon's native fish have been forced to spawn in a handful of smaller tributaries.

As spawning grounds have disappeared, so have the fish. Of the Canyon's eight native fish, four have gone extinct. Among those lost is the impressive six-foot Colorado squawfish. The humpback chub, one of the few species that remains, has been pushed to the brink of extinction. Scientists estimate that only a few thousand humpback chub remain in Grand Canyon. Adding to the problem are non-native sport fish that have been introduced to the river. New arrivals such as trout, catfish, and carp thrive in the chilly water and compete with native fish for resources.

Although the new Colorado has wreaked havoc with native fish populations, it has allowed other life forms to thrive. The cool, clear, sediment-free water allows sunlight to penetrate its depths, fostering the growth of algae. The abundance of algae has formed the foundation of a healthy food chain and turned the river a gorgeous shade of green.

Even the riverbank has undergone a major ecological change. For millions of years, the annual spring floods scoured the sides of the river. Now that flooding has been eliminated, a dense thicket of plants has taken up residence in the previous flood zone. This explosion of plants has led to a dramatic increase in animal habitat and biodiversity.

In the end, the construction of Glen Canyon Dam radically changed the ecology of the Colorado River in Grand Canyon. Although many conservationists would like to see the dam destroyed and the Colorado returned to its natural state, Glen Canyon Dam is unlikely to be decommissioned anytime soon. It provides valuable water and electricity to a desert region starved for both. And although the river's ecology has been shaken up, there have been some tangible improvements. The new river supports more plants and animals than the old one did, and its regulated flow allows hundreds of river trips to safely navigate Grand Canyon each year.

HUMAN HISTORY

ALTHOUGH THE COLORADO River is often hard to see from the rim of Grand Canyon, the Canyon itself is clearly visible from space. Equally impressive is the view from space at night when the desert is filled with dense clusters of light—the booming cities of the Southwest. Over the past few decades, millions of people have flocked to cities like Phoenix, Tucson and Las Vegas, eager to leave cold winters elsewhere behind. This phenomenal migration, continuing today, would have been impossible without water from the Colorado River. In a land of little rain, the Colorado is a river of liquid gold that has allowed the Southwest to flourish.

Today billions of dollars of agriculture, billions of dollars of industry, and millions of daily lives revolve around the Colorado River. Never before in history have so many people and such an enormous economy become so dependent on a single source of water. It is, without question, the most important natural resource in the West. But it is a limited resource, and huge demands have been placed on it. Today its flow is so regulated and its water so overused that not a single drop reaches the sea. And as the Southwest continues to grow, so do demands on the river. As a result, the Colorado has become one of the most argued over, litigated, politicized, and controversial rivers in the world.

The first attempt to tap the Colorado was a disaster. In the late 1800s, a developer named Charles Rockwood realized that, given a steady source of water, the California desert could be turned into an agricultural paradise. If the Colorado River could be tapped and controlled, farmers could grow crops an amazing 12 months of the year.

In 1901 a diversion channel was cut into the Colorado. Overnight, California's previously bone-dry Imperial Valley became one of the most productive agricultural regions on the planet. But because the Colorado ran thick with sediment, the diversion channel soon silted up and the Colorado jumped its banks, tearing off in a totally new direction. Instead of draining into the Gulf of California, the Colorado flowed into the middle of Southern California. For the next three years, the river dumped its entire flow into the desert lowland area known as the Salton Sink. By the time engineers were able to redirect the river, an inland sea roughly one-third the size of Rhode Island had formed. The Salton Sea is still there today.

The Colorado was a force to be reckoned with, but there was too much money at stake to give up trying to tame it. The arid West was on the verge of a massive expansion, and savvy politicians realized that its future was linked directly to water in the Colorado River. In the end, there was only one solution: build a massive dam that could regulate the Colorado, hold back its floods, and store them in a reservoir for later use.

In 1933 construction began on Hoover Dam. It was the biggest dam the world had ever seen. It tamed the Colorado, generated an enormous amount of electricity, and allowed the desert to bloom. Hoover Dam was such a resounding success that the government agency responsible for its creation, the Bureau of Reclamation, soon became the golden child of American politics. Using the momentum generated by Hoover Dam, the Bureau set off on a wild tear of dam building that lasted for the next 30 years.

The construction of so many expensive dams created huge economic windfalls in the states where they were built. Across the country, dam building was a politically charged process, but on the Colorado River the issue was even more complex. In 1922 a document called the Colorado River Compact had been drafted to allocate water from the Colorado River to the seven Colorado River Basin states. The Compact divided the region into an Upper Basin and a Lower Basin, each receiving 7.5 million acre feet of water per year. It was up to the states to figure out how to divvy up the water after that.

Not surprisingly, the Compact set off vicious inter-state water wars. Water was essential to each state's growth, and there simply wasn't enough to go around. The only way for a state to secure long-term water rights was to put that water to use before another state did. The result was the hasty construction of massive multi-billion dollar irrigation projects that, in reality, made little practical sense. In a few short decades, 19 dams had been built on the Colorado and its tributaries, and the river had been sucked dry.

Despite these problems, the Bureau of Reclamation continued to push for big new dams. In 1963 Glen Canyon Dam was constructed to the furor of conservationists. When two more dams were proposed within Grand Canyon, the conservationists went wild. Led by David Brower of the Sierra Club, they used congressional hearings, letter writing campaigns, and modern media savvy to defeat the dams (p.86).

The Bureau's defeat in Grand Canyon signaled a dramatic shift in popular opinion. Throughout much of the 20th century, dams had been viewed as glorious symbols of progress. But as the environmental movement took hold, many people viewed dams as hulking symbols of man's interference with nature. Before long, the era of massive dam building was brought to a halt.

The media blitz that defeated the dams also focused a tremendous amount of attention on the Colorado River in Grand Canyon. Soon, many ordinary people wanted to see it for themselves. Prior to 1950, fewer than 100 people had paddled through Grand Canyon. By 1970, roughly 15,000 people were making the trip each year. To reduce crowding, the park service began limiting the number of river runners allowed in Grand Canyon. Today roughly 20,000 people run the Colorado through Grand Canyon each year. And while the river as a whole is submerged in controversy, the uninterrupted stretch of whitewater in Grand Canyon remains one of the most rugged and beautiful places in the world.

THE COLORADO RIVER COMPACT

IN 1922 DELEGATES from seven western states gathered outside Santa Fe, New Mexico to allocate water from the Colorado River. Their negotiations resulted in the Colorado River Compact, which, at the time, was hailed as a "Constitution for the West." In reality, it was one of the most poorly conceived agreements in the history of American politics.

The Compact "solved" the issue of water ownership by splitting the Colorado River Basin into two: an Upper Basin (Utah, Wyoming, Colorado, New Mexico) and a Lower Basin (California, Arizona, Nevada). Of the estimated 17 million acre feet of water flowing through the Colorado River each year, each basin received 7.5 million acre feet, with Mexico receiving the remaining two million acre feet. The Compact left it up to the states to determine how the water was divided after that. Not surprisingly, the Colorado River Compact touched off vicious inter-state water wars. Tensions flared and relationships frayed, but the worst was yet to come.

In 1953 the government admitted there was a fatal flaw in the Colorado River Compact. The original document was written during a period of unusually high rainfall, and it *over*estimated the river's annual flow by roughly 3 million acre feet. States that had fought tooth and nail over every last drop of the Colorado River were now faced with the gut-wrenching fact that there was almost 20% less water than originally thought. The water wars grew even more heated, and they have remained so ever since.

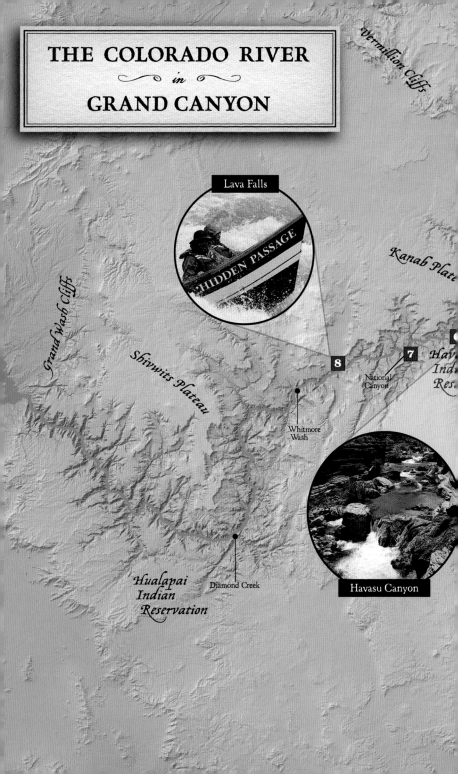

THE COLORADO RIVER
～ in ～
GRAND CANYON

Vermillion Cliffs

Lava Falls

HIDDEN PASSAGE

Kanab Platt

Grand Wash Cliffs

Shivwits Plateau

8

7 Hav
Ind
Res

National
Canyon

Whitmore
Wash

Hualapai
Indian
Reservation

Diamond Creek

Havasu Canyon

Marble Canyon

Shinumo Creek

Paria River

Lake Powell

1 Glen Canyon Dam

2 Lees Ferry

Navajo Indian Reservation

3 North Canyon

Marble Canyon

Redwall Cavern

Nankoweap

ánab anyon

Trinity Canyon

Blacktail Canyon

Saddle Canyon

4

Phantom Ranch

Bright Angel Point

Grand Canyon Village

Desert View

Little Colorado River

Coconino Plateau

Elves Chasm

Carbon Canyon

San Francisco Peaks

1 Glen Canyon Dam

This massive dam, located 15 river miles north of Grand Canyon, holds back Lake Powell—the largest man-made reservoir in the western hemisphere, capable of holding over eight trillion gallons of water. Glen Canyon Dam is 710 feet tall, 300 feet thick at the base, and contains over 4.9 million cubic yards of cement. It took seven years to build and cost $272 million in 1963 dollars. If the dam's eight generators operated at full capacity, the dam could release 15 million gallons of water a minute and generate roughly 1.3 million kilowatts of electricity.

Since Glen Canyon Dam went into operation in 1963, it has completely altered the downstream ecology of the Colorado River in Grand Canyon. For this reason, many conservationists loathe Glen Canyon Dam. In addition to the ecological changes it has wrought, the dam flooded Glen Canyon—by many accounts one of the most beautiful places in the Southwest. Supporters of the dam claim that Lake Powell is equally beautiful, and they point out that Glen Canyon Dam provides a steady source of clean, carbon-free energy.

But the attitudes of some former supporters have started to change. In 1997 former Arizona Senator Barry Goldwater, who originally supported the dam, came out against the dam in a PBS miniseries based on the book *Cadillac Desert*. "I have to be honest with you," he said, "I'd be happier if we didn't have the lake." Goldwater went on to say that, given the chance, "I'd vote against it. I've become convinced that, while water is important, particularly for those of us who live in the desert, it's not that important."

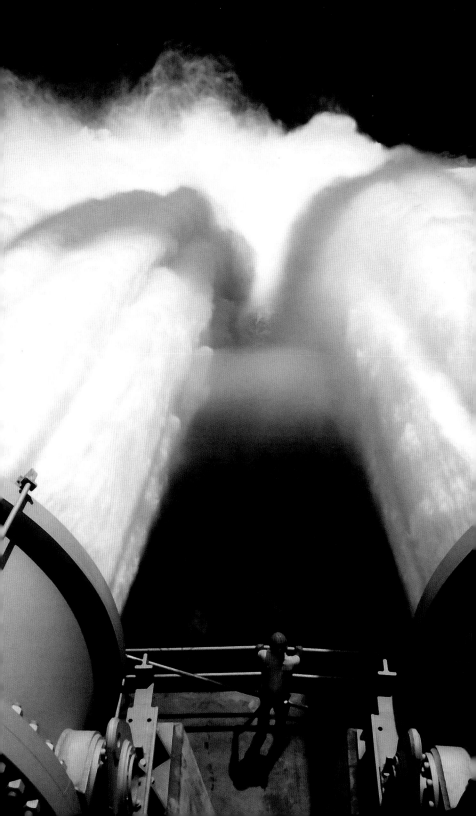

2 Lees Ferry (river mile 0)

Lees Ferry is the official launching point for every Grand Canyon river trip. It's the first spot on the Colorado River north of Grand Canyon accessible by road. (The next spot on the Colorado accessible by road is Diamond Creek, 225 miles downstream.) Lees Ferry is also the official boundary between the Upper and Lower Colorado River Basins, as set forth by the 1922 Colorado River Compact.

In 1776 Silvestre Vélez de Escalante, a Spanish missionary who became the first white person to set eyes on Lees Ferry, commented that, "It has an agreeably confused appearance." Despite being "agreeably confused," the gently sloping shores made it the only viable river crossing for hundreds of miles. For years, Lees Ferry was known as Paria Crossing, named after the Paria River that empties into the Colorado a short distance downstream. Then, in 1872, a Mormon named John D. Lee established a permanent ferry service here. A few years earlier, Lee had participated in the Mountain Meadows Massacre, in which a group of Mormons slaughtered a wagon train of 120 pioneers on their way to California. In 1870 Lee was excommunicated from the Mormon Church. With the law at his back, Lee fled to Grand Canyon. But just two years after establishing Lees Ferry, he was captured and brought to trial. In 1877 Lee was executed by firing squad at Mountain Meadows. The ferry service continued to operate until 1928, when a ferry carrying a Model T capsized and killed all three people aboard. The following year, Navajo Bridge was constructed a few miles downstream.

▨3 Marble Canyon (river miles 0–61)

Marble Canyon gives river runners their first taste of the power and beauty of Grand Canyon. Its steep, narrow walls offer dramatic scenery broken up by dozens of exciting rapids. Ironically, there's no marble in Marble Canyon. The name was given by John Wesley Powell, who thought the sedimentary rocks— polished smooth by muddy river water—resembled marble.

In the 1960s, the U.S. Bureau of Reclamation wanted to build a dam at river mile 39. Had the dam been built, the upper reaches of Marble Canyon would have been flooded, but public pressure ultimately defeated the Bureau's plan.

> **WE HAVE CUT** through the sandstones and limestones met in the upper part of the canyon, and through one great bed of marble a thousand feet in thickness. In this, great numbers of caves are hollowed out, and carvings are seen which suggest architectural forms, though on a scale so grand that architectural terms belittle them. As this great bed forms a distinctive feature of the canyon, we call it Marble Canyon.
>
> —John Wesley Powell

VASEY'S PARADISE

This beautiful spring gushes forth from a cave in the Redwall Limestone. As John Wesley Powell noted, "We find fountains bursting from the rock high overhead, and the spray in the sunshine forms the gems which bedeck the wall. The rocks below the fountain are covered with mosses and ferns and many beautiful flowering plants. We name it Vasey's Paradise, in honor of the botanist who traveled with us last year." Grand Canyon's Redwall Limestone is riddled with caves and aquifers, including one that feeds Vasey's Paradise. The lush vegetation here supports eight species of mollusks, including the endangered, inch-long Kanab ambersnail.

THE WATER SWEEPS rapidly in this elbow of river, and has cut its way under the rock, excavating a vast half-circular chamber, which, if utilized for a theater, would give seating to 50,000 people. Objection might be raised against it, however, for at high water the floor is covered with a raging flood."

—John Wesley Powell

Redwall Cavern

North Canyon

Saddle Canyon

4 Nankoweap (river mile 53)

Nankoweap is considered by many to be Marble Canyon's most beautiful stretch of river. In addition to spectacular scenery, this graceful bend in the river offers famous archaeological sites, pristine camping, and spectacular hiking nearby.

The origin of the name Nankoweap is a bit of a mystery. Some scholars believe the word is derived from a Paiute phrase meaning "Place Where Two Tribes Fought." Others believe the phrase means "Place That Echoes." What is known is that Nankoweap was home to an Ancestral Puebloan settlement hundreds of years ago. These ancient people, predecessors of the modern Hopi and Navajo tribes, farmed the fertile delta at Nankoweap and built granaries (stone storage compartments) in the cliffs above.

AND WHAT A world of grandeur is spread before us! Below is the canyon through which the Colorado runs ... Away to the west are lines of cliffs and ledges of rock—not such ledges as the reader may have seen where the quarryman splits his blocks, but ledges from which the gods might quarry mountains ...

—John Wesley Powell

Nankoweap

Trinity Canyon

Shinumo Creek

Elves Chasm

Blacktail Canyon

Deer Creek Falls

"The clouds are children of the heavens, and when they play among the rocks they lift them to the region above."

—John Wesley Powell

Deer Creek Narrows

Deer Creek Narrows

5 Kanab Canyon (river mile 143)

Kanab Canyon is one of Grand Canyon's largest and most beautiful side canyons. It was named by John Wesley Powell after the Paiute word for "willow." In 1872 Powell and his men ended their second Colorado River expedition here, hiking out of the Canyon to the North Rim. One year earlier, two prospectors had discovered trace amounts of gold in Kanab Canyon, setting off a minor gold rush that brought hundreds of fortune seekers here. The gold rush—which lasted all of four months—ended when the eager prospectors finally accepted the fact that there were no sizeable gold deposits in Kanab Canyon.

THE CREVICES ARE usually narrow above and, by erosion of the streams, wider below, forming a network of caves, each cave having a narrow, winding skylight up through the rocks. Wherever we look there is but a wilderness of rocks—deep gorges where the rivers are lost below cliffs and towers and pinnacles, and ten thousand strangely carved forms in every direction...

—John Wesley Powell

6 Havasu Canyon (river mile 157)

The beauty of Grand Canyon is stunning, but the beauty of Havasu Canyon seems almost hallucinatory. This secluded oasis—the most abundant side stream in Grand Canyon—is part tropical paradise, part Southwestern dreamscape. A well-worn path heads up Havasu Canyon from the river, revealing shockingly turquoise water tumbling over pink rocks in a series of tranquil pools, each one more beautiful than the last. No matter how far up the path you go, you'll be greeted with some of the most incredible scenery in the Southwest.

Havasu Canyon is located on the Havasupai Indian Reservation. Follow the path up Havasu Canyon 10 miles and you'll reach the village of Supai, home to about 450 members of the Havasupai tribe. *Havasupai*, loosely translated, means "People of the Blue Green Water." Supai's world-famous waterfalls draw several thousand visitors a year, but the village, located 2,000 feet below the rim, is only accessible by foot, mule or helicopter (p.283). Although it's unrealistic to hike from the river to Supai and back in a single day, Beaver Falls (located about four miles up the trail) is a beautiful waterfall that makes a good destination for strong day hikers.

Havasu Canyon only receives nine inches of rain a year, but it drains a 3,000 square-mile basin. That drainage, combined with a gushing spring, provides Havasu Creek with an average of 38 million gallons of water a day. The vivid blue water is due to dissolved calcium carbonate and magnesium, which gives the water its otherworldly hue.

Beaver Falls, Havasu Canyon

7 National Canyon (river mile 166)

National Canyon is one of many exquisite side canyons branching off from the Colorado River. These canyons, carved out over millions of years by flash floods roaring down from the rim, offer some of the most amazing scenery in Grand Canyon. Their walls have been sculpted and polished in an endless variety of patterns, alternately catching and concealing the sunlight throughout the day. Many of these side canyons are accessible only from the river, making them the exclusive domain of river runners. Some go on for miles, offering incredible hiking that many river runners consider to be the best part of the trip.

THE GORGE IS black and narrow below, red and gray and flaring above, with crags and angular projections on the walls, which, cut in many places by side canyons, seem to be a vast wilderness of rocks ... and ever as we go there is some new pinnacle or tower, some crag or peak, some distant view of the upper plateau, some strangely shaped rock, or some deep, narrow side canyon.

—John Wesley Powell

Matkatamiba Canyon

Matkatamiba Canyon

"**W**hat a conflict of water and fire there must have been here! Just imagine a river of molten rock running down into a river of melted snow. What a seething and boiling of the waters; what clouds of steam rolled into the heavens."

—John Wesley Powell

8 Lava Falls (river mile 179)

Lava Falls is one of the most challenging, terrifying, and thrilling rapids in Grand Canyon. It drops 13 feet in a matter of seconds, providing river runners with a rip-roaring ride—regardless of whether or not you stay inside your boat. Lava Falls is also the last major rapid conquered on most river trips—the grand finale after a symphony of singular sights.

Lava Falls is named for the nearby lava flows that have tumbled over the rim several times over the past 2 million years, accounting for the dark-colored basalt on the north side of the river. Roughly 1.6 million years ago, a nearby volcanic eruption sent four cubic miles of lava tumbling down to the Colorado River. When the lava cooled, it plugged the Canyon and formed a dam at least 2,300 feet high, creating a reservoir that took 22 years to fill and stretched all the way back to Moab, Utah.

Lava Falls shows mercy to no man, as demonstrated in 1989 when the rapids flipped a boat carrying Hollywood heavyweights Tom Cruise, Jeffrey Katzenberg, and Don Simpson. In the late 1980s, private Grand Canyon "power trips" became popular among Tinseltown titans and movie execs. The luxury on these trips was so extravagant, so over the top, so beyond anything the Canyon had ever seen that they are still talked about to this day. As the moguls conquered the rapids, extra supply rafts tagged along carrying gourmet food, wine, white linens, fine china, assistants, and private chefs. At night, candlelight dinners were served on the banks of the Colorado, featuring delicacies such as caviar and live lobster.

Lava Falls

THE NORTH RIM

★ ★ ★ ★ ★

THE NORTH RIM

THE NORTH RIM lies just 10 miles from the South Rim as the condor flies, but those of us confined to the ground have to drive 200 miles *around* Grand Canyon to get there. Make no mistake, the North Rim is remote. The closest major airport, Las Vegas' McCarran, is 280 miles to the southwest, and traveling to the North Rim means driving through one of the least densely populated places in the continental United States. As a result, fewer than one in ten Grand Canyon visitors ever make it to the North Rim. But those who do are rewarded with limited crowds and some of Grand Canyon's most spectacular views. As a result, it's one of my favorite places in the park.

The North Rim is 1,000 feet higher than the South Rim, resulting in cooler temperatures and 60 percent more precipitation. Because of the cool and wet climate, the North Rim is covered in alpine forests of spruce, fir and aspen, giving it a feel more like the Rockies than the desert Southwest. During summer heat spells, when the South Rim is sweltering, the North Rim enjoys balmy afternoons and mild summer nights. Winters, on the other hand, bring so much snow that AZ-67—the only road to the North Rim—is forced to shut down. Only cross country skiers and snowshoers are allowed in the park during this time.

The hub of all activity on the North Rim is Grand Canyon Lodge (p.262), located at the southern terminus of AZ-67. The lodge offers overnight accommodations on the rim, but even if you're not a guest you can relax on the open-air back porch or dine in the upscale restaurant, both of which offer spectacular Canyon views. A short distance away is the pristine North Rim Campground, which fills up fast in the summer. Both the lodge and the campground are located within walking distance of Bright Angel Point (p.261), the North Rim's most popular overlook. A lazy drive along Cape Royal Road, meanwhile, brings you to even more spectacular views at Cape Royal (p.265) and Point Imperial (p.264) along the Walhalla Plateau.

The North Rim doesn't have an extensive selection of restaurants or gift shops, but that's all part of its charm. Visitors here are more interested in the rugged scenery and the plentiful day hikes along the rim. If you're looking for a challenging overnight hike, the North Kaibab Trail (p.274) descends 14 miles to Bright Angel Campground and Phantom Ranch.

North Rim
BASICS

Getting to the North Rim

There's only one road to Grand Canyon's North Rim: AZ-67, which heads south from the small town of Jacob Lake on I-89A. From Jacob Lake follow AZ-67 44 miles south to the park entrance. From the park entrance it's an additional 13 miles to Grand Canyon Lodge. No buses or trains run to the North Rim, but there are private shuttles that makes regular runs between the South Rim and the North Rim (see below). The closest major airports are located in Las Vegas, Nevada (280 miles, 5 hours driving), and Salt Lake City, Utah (380 miles, 7 hours driving). There is also limited air service to the small town of St. George, Utah (150 miles, 3 hours driving) from Salt Lake City.

RIM TO RIM SHUTTLES

From mid-May through mid-October, private shuttles runs daily trips between the North Rim and the South Rim. The drive lasts about five hours each way. **Trans-Canyon Shuttle** (928-638-2820, www.trans-canyonshuttle.com) leaves the North Rim at 7am and arrives at the South Rim around noon. It then leaves the South Rim at 1:30pm and arrives back at the North Rim around 6pm. Cost: $85 one-way, $160 round-trip. **The Grand Canyon Shuttle** runs two shuttles leaving the South Rim and North Rim at 7:30am and arriving at their respective destinations around 11:30am. The shuttles then leave the North Rim and South Rim at 2pm and arrives at their respective destinations around 6:30pm. Cost: $85 one-way, $160 round-trip. (928-606-9212, www.thegrandcanyonshuttle.com)

Information

The best resource for North Rim information is the North Rim edition of the park's free newspaper, *The Guide*. Copies of *The Guide* are handed out at the park entrance station. Information is also available at the North Rim Visitor Center (open 8am to 6pm), adjacent to Grand Canyon Lodge, which features a ranger-staffed help desk, maps, brochures, exhibits and a well-stocked bookstore. The U.S. Forest Service also operates the Kaibab Plateau Visitor Center (open 8am–5pm) near the junction of I-89A and AZ-67.

Fees

The North Rim entrance fee (which also gives you access to the South Rim) is $25 per vehicle or $12 per pedestrian, motorcycle rider or cyclist. Admission is good for seven days. There's also an annual pass to Grand Canyon ($50) and the America The Beautiful Pass ($80), which gives you unlimited access to all U.S. national parks and federal recreation lands for one full year.

Weather & When to Go

Winter dumps an average of 12 feet of snow on the North Rim, closing the park's only access road, AZ-67. The road reopens in the spring when the snow melts, generally around mid-May. Spring is delightful, but the weather can be unpredictable. Pack warm clothes and be prepared for sudden temperature changes.

Summer is the busiest time on the North Rim, but the crowds are rarely excessive. Due to its high elevation, the North Rim is about five to ten degrees cooler than the South Rim, which means summer temperatures are generally divine. That said, afternoon thundershowers are common during "monsoon season," which lasts from July through early September.

Fall is a beautiful time on the North Rim, with sparse crowds and gorgeous foliage, but be prepared for cold temperatures at night. North Rim facilities shut down in mid-October, but the park remains open until winter's first heavy snow, which often occurs around mid-November. When snowfall closes AZ-67, the park is open only to adventurous snowshoers and cross country skiers.

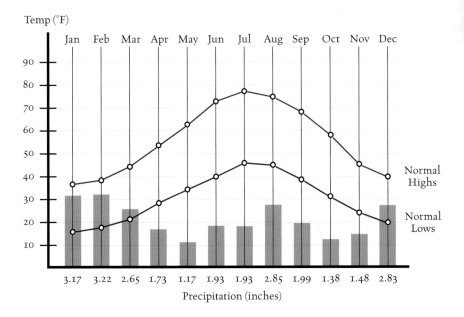

Temp (°F)

| | Jan | Feb | Mar | Apr | May | Jun | Jul | Aug | Sep | Oct | Nov | Dec |

Precipitation (inches): 3.17 3.22 2.65 1.73 1.17 1.93 1.93 2.85 1.99 1.38 1.48 2.83

Normal Highs

Normal Lows

Getting Around the North Rim

It's entirely possible to have a great time on the North Rim without your own set of wheels, but having a car or bike is essential if you want to explore any part of the North Rim not within walking distance of Grand Canyon Lodge. The dramatic Walhalla Plateau, which offers some of the best viewpoints and day hikes in the park, is 13 miles from the lodge by road. Note that bicycles are allowed on all paved and dirt roads on the North Rim (unless otherwise posted), but they are prohibited from all other park trails.

Unlike the bustling South Rim, the North Rim does not offer regular shuttle service. The only shuttle on the North Rim is the early morning North Rim Hiker Shuttle, which runs between Grand Canyon Lodge and the North Kaibab Trailhead. The shuttle picks passengers up in front of the lodge at 5:45am and 7:10am. Cost: $7 per person. Tickets available at the front desk of the lodge and reservations are recommended 24 hours in advance.

What to Bring

Unlike the bustling South Rim, shopping at the North Rim is very limited, so proper packing is essential. The weather can turn on a dime, so make sure you bring plenty of warm clothes and rain gear. And if you're camping, make sure you bring all the food and cooking equipment you need. The North Rim's general store has a decent selection of food and camping equipment, but they sometimes run out of essentials during peak season.

Dining

★ THE LODGE DINING ROOM (Brk: $7–8; Lnch: $10–14; Din: $17–25)

This grand restaurant offers the best dining on the North Rim. The menu is decidedly Western, but classed up with Italian and French touches. The atmosphere is rustic/elegant, and the views of the Canyon are tremendous. Dinner reservations are required. (928-638-2612)

DELI IN THE PINES (Lnch, Din: $7–10)

This cafeteria-style restaurant, located on the west side of Grand Canyon Lodge, offers basic sandwiches, hot dogs, pizza ($15–20), and a few healthy options like fresh fruits and salads. The interior is bland, so grab your food and head to the lodge's gorgeous outdoor terraces.

ROUGH RIDER SALOON

This Western-themed saloon is an early morning coffee shop by day, and a well-stocked bar by night. Pizza slices and light appetizers are also served. Located on the east side of Grand Canyon Lodge.

Lodging
GRAND CANYON LODGE

This rustic lodge is perched right on the rim of the Canyon, and it offers the park's only overnight accommodations on the North Rim. Motel-style rooms and private cabins are available, but both are often booked months in advance during the summer. Rates: $124–192. (888-297-2757, www.grandcanyonlodgenorth.com)

Camping
NORTH RIM CAMPGROUND

This pristine campground, located about a mile northwest of Grand Canyon Lodge, has about 90 sites, four with Canyon views. Rate: $18 ($25 for the four sites with Canyon views); backpackers and other visitors without cars only pay $4 per night. Reservations, which can be made up to six months in advance, are highly recommended. (877-444-6777, www.recreation.gov)

Gas, Supplies & Services

Just past the turnoff to the North Rim Campground there's small gas station with 24-hour pumps. Continue down the road and you'll see a shower house with coin-operated showers and a coin-operated laundry on your right. Just beyond the shower house, next to the campground entrance, is the North Rim General Store, which sells basic groceries, beer, wine and camping supplies.

Activities
RANGER PROGRAMS

Free ranger programs are offered daily on topics including history, geology, wildlife and more. Check *The Guide* for seasonal times and locations.

MULE RIDES

Day trips are offered along the rim and partway down the North Kaibab Trail. One-hour trips ($40) and half-day trips ($80) are offered. For more information, visit the Grand Canyon Trail Rides desk at Grand Canyon Lodge. (435-679-8665)

GRAND CANYON STAR PARTY

Grand Canyon boasts some of the darkest skies left in the continental U.S., and local astronomy clubs celebrate this fact each June by setting up telescopes for the public on the North Rim. Exact dates vary depending on the new moon.

AMERICAN INDIAN HERITAGE DAYS

For two decades the Kaibab Band of Paiute Indians have been celebrating their native culture with a series of events held in early August.

OUTSIDE THE PARK

AZ-67, which connects the small town of Jacob Lake to the park, is home to a handful of restaurants, lodges and campgrounds. If you're interested in exploring the Kaibab National Forest, which surrounds most of AZ-67, visit the Kaibab Plateau Ranger Station in Jacob Lake.

Lodging

KAIBAB LODGE

Located six miles north of the park entrance (19 miles north of park visitor center), this collection of stand-alone cabins is a good alternative if all the rooms at Grand Canyon Lodge are booked. Rates: $90-185. (928-638-2389, www.kaibablodge.com)

JACOB LAKE INN

Located 31 miles north of the park entrance (44 miles north of park visitor center), the Jacob Lake Inn offers a combination of motel rooms and private cabins. Rates: $90-140. (928-643-7232, www.jacoblake.com)

Camping

DEMOTTE CAMPGROUND

This 38-site campground is located six miles north of the park entrance in the Kaibab National Forest. Cost: $18 per night. (877-444-6777, www.recreation.gov)

JACOB LAKE CAMPGROUND

This 51-site campground is located 31 miles north of the park entrance in Jacob Lake. Cost: $18 per night. (877-444-6777, www.recreation.gov)

Dining

JACOB LAKE INN (Brk: $6-9; Lnch: $8-10, Din $18-21)

Hearty food in a cozy atmosphere. Their house specialty, Kaibab Jagerschnitzel, is a pork cutlet grilled with bacon and juniper berries. (928-643-7232)

KAIBAB LODGE RESTAURANT (Brk: $7-8; Lnch: $8-10, Din $10-20)

This rustic restaurant serves breakfast classics, sandwiches, burgers, soups and steaks. Located six miles north of the park entrance on AZ-67. (928-638-2389)

Gas & Supplies

A Chevron station in Jacob Lake offers 24-hour pumps, and the Jacob Lake Inn next door has a small convenience store with homemade baked goods. About 25 miles south of Jacob Lake on AZ-67 is the North Rim Country Store, which sells basic groceries, beer firewood and gas from 7:30am to 7pm.

North Rim Foliage

Aspen trees grow on the cool, high Kaibab Plateau, and in late September/ early October their leaves turn a magnificent shade of gold. In recent years the foliage has become even more dramatic due to a series of fires in the early 2000s. The fires burned over 75,000 acres on the Kaibab Plateau, killing thousands of tall ponderosa pines that had previously dominated the landscape. Sun-loving aspen flourished in the new open spaces, and they are now the dominant tree species in many places. Decades from now ponderosa pines will once again reclaim the landscape, but until then autumn on the North Rim promises to be particularly beautiful.

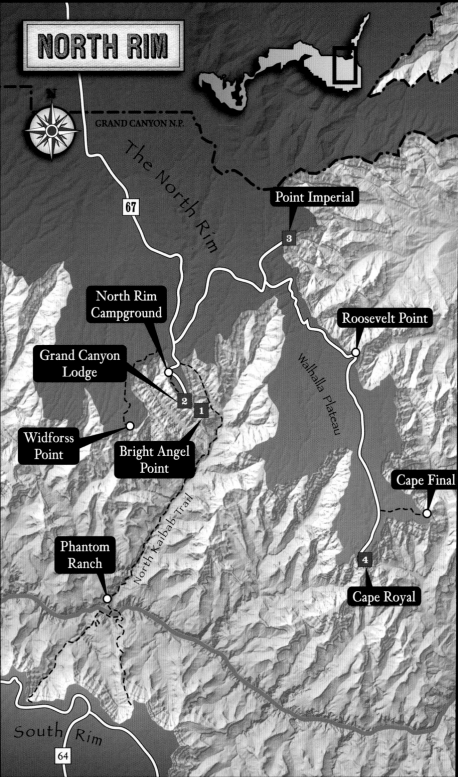

NORTH RIM

GRAND CANYON N.P.

The North Rim

67

Point Imperial

3

North Rim
Campground

Roosevelt Point

Grand Canyon
Lodge

Walhalla Plateau

2

1

Widforss
Point

Bright Angel
Point

Cape Final

North Kaibab Trail

Phantom
Ranch

4

Cape Royal

South Rim

64

1 Bright Angel Point

This popular viewpoint, located southeast of Grand Canyon Lodge, is accessible via a short paved path that begins to the left of the North Rim Visitor Center, just beyond the cabin area. After an initial drop at the start, the trail stays relatively flat with only a few mild ups and downs. Dramatic views of Roaring Springs Canyon unfold to your left, and towards the end of the trail you'll come to a small bridge that takes you to Bright Angel Point. The point itself is fenced in by a small metal railing. Interpretive signs point out famous Canyon landmarks visible from Bright Angel Point. The rocky outcrop directly behind the observation platform is a popular place to take in the view, but use caution if you climb onto the outcrop.

Gazing across the Canyon from Bright Angel Point, the walls of the South Rim appear nearly vertical. The walls of the North Rim, meanwhile, gradually recede from the Colorado River. This stark contrast is due to varying rates of erosion. Both the North Rim and the South Rim are tilted slightly to the south, so any precipitation that falls on the North Rim flows *into* the Canyon, while any precipitation that falls on the South Rim flows *away* from the Canyon. Because the walls of the North Rim receive so much more runoff, they have eroded horizontally up to *10 times* faster than the walls of the South Rim.

Beyond the South Rim, dotting the southeastern horizon, are the San Francisco Mountains. On clear days you can make out Humphrey's Peak, the highest point in Arizona at 12,643 feet.

2 Grand Canyon Lodge

Perched right on the rim, Grand Canyon Lodge offers tremendous views of the Canyon from its two open-air terraces. During the day, these terraces are great places to relax and take in the views. At night, a fire often crackles in the stone fireplace on the eastern terrace. Sandwiched between the terraces is the indoor Sun Room, where comfy leather chairs face giant picture windows that gaze out over the Canyon. The Sun Room is a great place to watch the summer monsoon storms. It's also home to a bronze statue of Brighty the Mule (rub his nose for good luck), and over the fireplace is a large statue of a Hopi Tihu (p.61). Several spectacular Navajo Rugs are also draped around the lodge.

The original Grand Canyon Lodge, built in 1928, was the brainchild of Stephen Mather, the first director of the National Park Service. In the 1920s Mather championed the construction of grand lodges in national parks. Beautiful lodges helped lure visitors to national parks, which, in turn, justified the existence of the fledgling National Park Service. Designed by Gilbert Stanley Underwood— the architect behind Yosemite's famous Ahwahnee Hotel—the original Grand Canyon Lodge was built out of native ponderosa pines and Kaibab limestone. But just four years after it opened, the original structure burned down in a tragic fire. Only the small buildings on either side of the structure were spared, and they are still in use today. The current lodge was built in 1936. When completed it boasted improvements such as steel beams (as opposed to flammable pine beams) and sloped roofs to deflect the North Rim's heavy snows.

③ Point Imperial

At 8,803 feet, Point Imperial is the highest viewpoint in Grand Canyon and the best sunrise spot on the North Rim. To get there by car from Grand Canyon Lodge, drive north three miles on AZ-67 and then turn right onto Fuller Canyon Road. When the road forks, turn left and follow the road until you reach a large parking area. Park your car and follow the obvious path down to the dramatic viewpoint below.

The prominent spire in front of the viewpoint marks the top of Mount Hayden (8,372 feet). The spire is composed of Coconino Sandstone, the third youngest rock layer in Grand Canyon, which formed roughly 265 million years ago when Northern Arizona was covered with massive sand dunes similar to today's Sahara Desert. Over millions of years, those sand dunes were buried and compressed into sandstone. Thus, when you stare out at Mount Hayden, you're actually staring at the compressed remains of 265 million-year-old sand dunes!

Beyond Mount Hayden, the view stretches out for miles, offering one of the best panoramas in the park. To the left of Mount Hayden, the Colorado River flows through Marble Canyon (p.216) before reaching the confluence of the Little Colorado River (distinguished by a deep side canyon stretching east). Above Marble Canyon is a broad, flat platform marking the westernmost edge of the Painted Desert, which stretches 150 miles southeast to Petrified Forest National Park. Almost all visible land east of Marble Canyon belongs to the Navajo Nation, which, at 27,425 square miles, is the largest Indian Reservation in the U.S.

4 Walhalla Plateau

This dramatic "sky peninsula" juts out 15 miles into the Canyon just east of Bright Angel Point and contains some of the North Rim's finest and most accessible scenery. To get to Walhalla Plateau by car from Grand Canyon Lodge, drive north three miles on AZ-67 and then turn right onto Fuller Canyon Road. When the road forks, turn right onto Cape Royal Road, which heads to Cape Royal at the southern tip of the plateau.

As you head to Cape Royal, you'll pass a number of interesting viewpoints including Vista Encantada ("Enchanting View") and Roosevelt Point, which provides a rare glimpse of the confluence of the Colorado and Little Colorado Rivers. Cape Final (p.268) is a short, highly recommended day hike that starts six miles past Roosevelt Point. Continue to Walhalla Overlook, which offers a view of Unkar Delta (p.162) next to the Colorado River. Across the road from Walhalla Overlook are the faint remains of a nine-room Ancestral Puebloan home, probably inhabited around A.D. 1050. Back then there were over 100 seasonal farming sites on the Walhalla Plateau where beans, corn, and squash were grown.

Cape Royal Road ends at a large parking area. From the parking area, a short paved trail passes by Angel's Arch, a natural arch that frames a view of the Colorado River and heads to Cape Royal. Curving out in front of Cape Royal are the dramatic cliffs of Wotans Throne. Although seemingly inaccessible, an exploring party in the 1930s discovered archaeological evidence indicating that Native Americans once lived on top of Wotans Throne.

◁ TRANSEPT TRAIL ▷

SUMMARY   The Transept Trail is an easy, charming stroll along the dramatic edge of Transept Canyon. Connecting Grand Canyon Lodge with the North Rim Campground, the trail treats hikers to dramatic Canyon views and shady rambles among ponderosa pines. If you feel like stretching out your legs but don't feel like working up a sweat, this is the trail for you. Benches are set up at several points, offering terrific views of Bright Angel Point, Bright Angel Canyon, and the many temples beyond. Along the way, you'll also pass a small Ancestral Puebloan ruin. In the early morning, the Transept Trail is a great place to see wildlife such as mule deer, chipmunks, and squirrels. Bird watchers should also keep an eye out for wrens, juncos, and woodpeckers.

TRAILHEAD   From Grand Canyon Lodge: Head down the obvious trail towards Bright Angel Point and turn right off the pavement after one-tenth of a mile. From the North Rim Campground: Head west from the general store and look for the sign that marks the trail.

TRAIL INFO

RATING: Easy   **HIKING TIME:** 45 minutes

DISTANCE: 3 miles, round-trip   **ELEVATION CHANGE:** 100 ft.

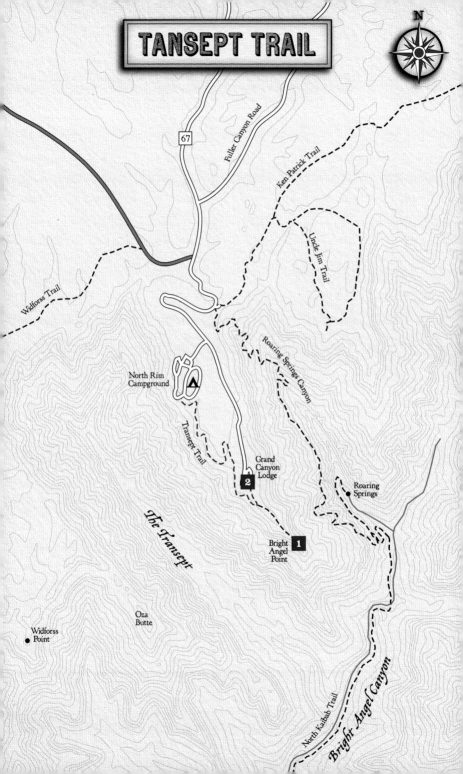

‿ CAPE FINAL TRAIL ‿

SUMMARY   This highly recommended hike heads to the easternmost tip of Walhalla Plateau, offering sweeping views of the Vishnu Temple, Jupiter Temple, and eastern Grand Canyon. The views are among the finest on the North Rim, and due to Cape Final's relatively remote location crowds are generally few and far between. From Cape Royal Road, the trail heads through an open ponderosa forest, then strolls past cacti and pinyon pines. Cape Final itself, reached via a faint path, can be a bit hard to find—look for the USGS datum points embedded in the bedrock at the overlook. Backpacking note: It's possible to camp at Cape Final. The park's Backcountry Office grants one camping permit per night. If you're lucky enough to get your hands on that permit, you'll have Cape Final all to yourself at night!

TRAILHEAD   The Cape Final Trail starts along Cape Royal Road. The small trailhead (which can be easy to miss) starts roughly 11.8 miles south of the junction with Point Imperial Road (2.5 miles north of the end of Cape Royal Road).

TRAIL INFO

RATING: Easy   **HIKING TIME:** 2 hours

DISTANCE: 4 miles, round-trip   **ELEVATION CHANGE:** 150 ft.

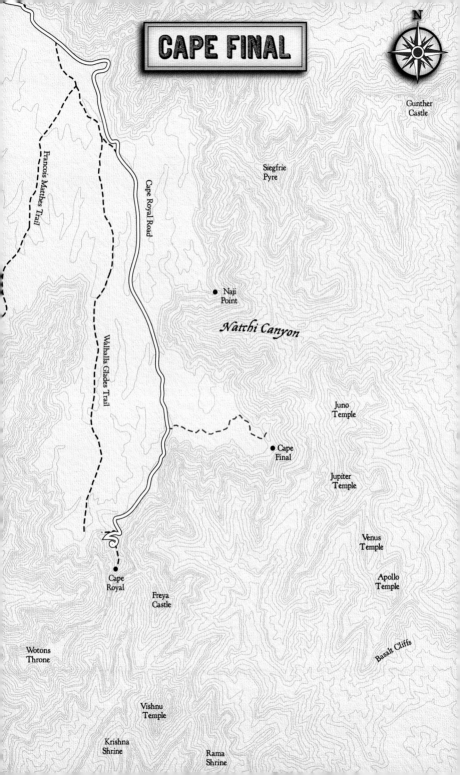

ᴧ CLIFF SPRING TRAIL ᴦ

SUMMARY   This easy trail, located near the southern tip of the Walhalla Plateau, rambles along a steep, forested ravine to a small spring. About 100 yards past the trailhead is an Ancestral Puebloan granary, used roughly 1,000 years ago to store crops such as beans, corn and squash. Beyond the granary, the trail drops down and wraps around some striking 30-foot cliffs with a pronounced overhang. Soon you'll reach a peaceful rock alcove filled with lush vegetation where you can see Cliff Spring squeezing itself out of the rock. (Note: Do not drink the water, which may be contaminated.) A rugged trail continues past Cliff Spring, providing dramatic views as the steep ravine plummets into Grand Canyon.

TRAILHEAD   The Cliff Spring Trail starts on the inside of a hairpin turn about half a mile from the end of Cape Royal Road (roughly 13.5 miles south of the junction with Point Imperial Road). Parking is available at a pullover on the left side of the road. A signed trailhead is located across the street.

◀ TRAIL INFO ▶

RATING: Easy

DISTANCE: 1 mile, round-trip

HIKING TIME: 1 hour

ELEVATION CHANGE: 200 ft.

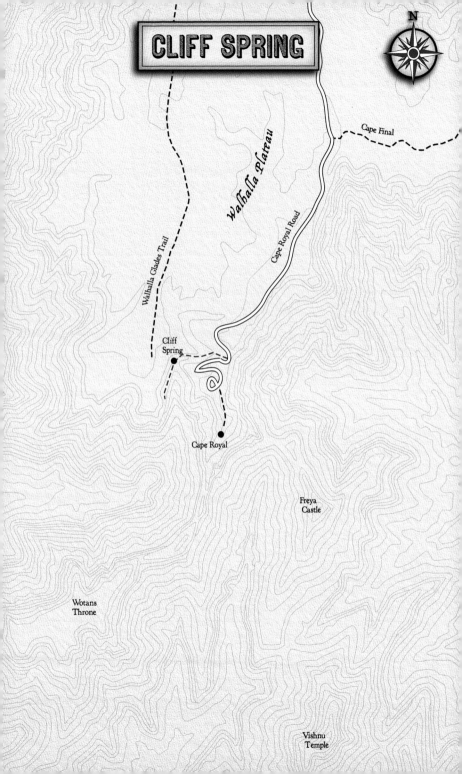

⇜ WIDFORSS TRAIL ⇝

SUMMARY   This long hike skirts the northwestern edge of the Transept, then cuts through the forest to Widforss Point. For lovers of wildflowers and woodland scenery, the Widforss Trail has few rivals on the North Rim. After a quick climb at the start, the trail skirts the forested rim of the Transept. Numbered posts correspond to points of interest listed in a brochure available at the trailhead. Eventually the trail veers away from the rim and heads through the forest. The trail narrows towards the end, reaching an old picnic table before dropping down to Widforss Point, which offers sweeping Canyon views. Both Widforss Point and the Widforss Trail were named in honor of artist Gunnar M. Widforss, who painted vivid watercolors of Grand Canyon in the 1920s and 1930s. Backpacking note: Camping permits are available for the Widforss Trail.

TRAILHEAD   From Grand Canyon Lodge, drive north on AZ-67 for about 2.5 miles until you see a sign for the turnoff to Widforss Point. Turn left onto the dirt road and follow it for about half a mile. There is a signed parking area for the Widforss Trail on the left. The trail starts on the south side of the parking area.

◗ TRAIL INFO ◖

RATING: Moderate   **HIKING TIME:** 4–5 hours

DISTANCE: 10 miles, round-trip   **ELEVATION CHANGE:** 400 ft.

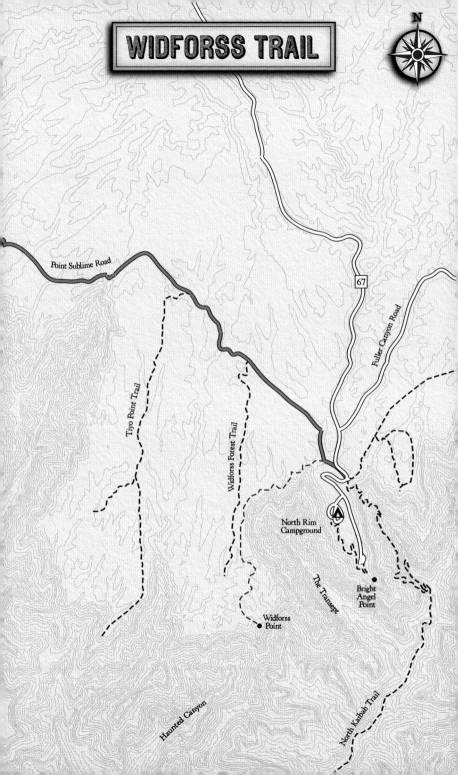

⊰ NORTH KAIBAB TRAIL ⊱

SUMMARY   The steep, strenuous North Kaibab Trail is the only maintained trail on the North Rim that descends into the Canyon. Though physically demanding, it offers a tremendous Inner Canyon experience, passing through a stunning range of ecological zones. Backpackers typically spend three to four days hiking the trail, spending the night at Cottonwood Campground (halfway down the trail) and Bright Angel Campground (located near the Colorado River). Day hikers can head to Coconino Overlook (1.5 miles, round-trip) or Supai Tunnel (4 miles, round-trip). Two beautiful waterfalls, Roaring Springs and Ribbon Falls, are accessible via short side trails much farther down the trail. Towards the end of the trail, you'll pass through The Box—a narrow, shady corridor that twists along Bright Angel Creek through 1.7 billion-year-old Vishnu Schist.

TRAILHEAD   The trail starts about two miles north of Grand Canyon Lodge just off AZ-67. A small parking area is located next to the trailhead. There's also a free early morning shuttle that departs from Grand Canyon Lodge (p.256).

TRAIL INFO

RATING: Strenuous

DISTANCE: 28 miles, round-trip

HIKING TIME: 3–4 Days

ELEVATION CHANGE: 5,850 ft.

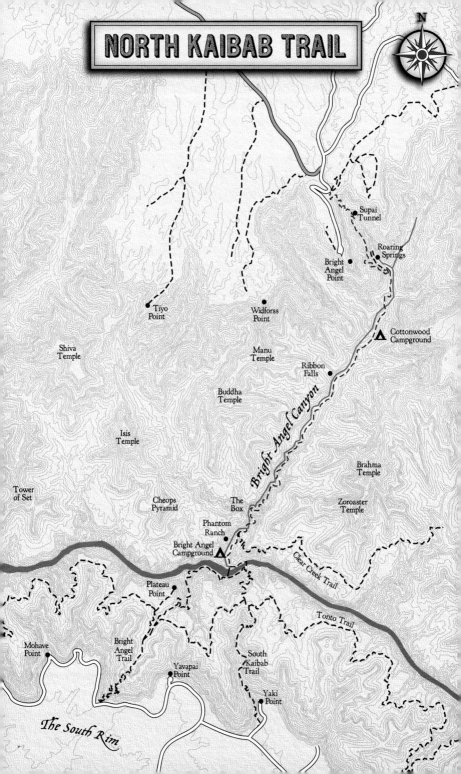

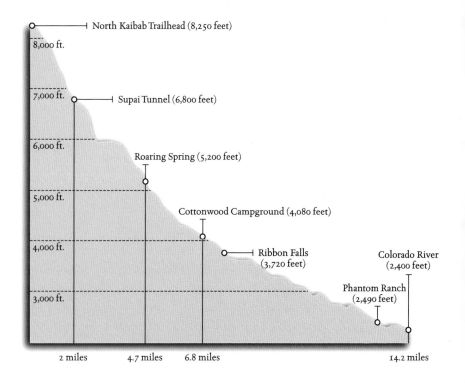

North Kaibab Trailhead (8,250 feet)

8,000 ft.

7,000 ft. — Supai Tunnel (6,800 feet)

6,000 ft.

Roaring Spring (5,200 feet)

5,000 ft.

Cottonwood Campground (4,080 feet)

4,000 ft.

Ribbon Falls (3,720 feet)

Colorado River (2,400 feet)

Phantom Ranch (2,490 feet)

3,000 ft.

2 miles　　4.7 miles　　6.8 miles　　14.2 miles

NORTH KAIBAB TRAIL

Ribbon Falls

TOROWEAP

Toroweap (AKA Tuweep) is a rugged North Rim campground that's home to one of Grand Canyon's most spectacular views. From an elevation of 4,552 feet at the rim, sheer cliffs drop 3,000 vertical feet to the Colorado River. The distance from rim to rim is less than a mile, making this one of the narrowest and deepest places in Grand Canyon. Despite the stunning views, few visitors ever make it to Toroweap due to its remote location (35 miles west of Jacob Lake), rugged approach, and lack of modern amenities. But for those hardy travelers that do make it here, the lack of luxury is exactly the point.

Just west of Toroweap, dark rocks mark the path of ancient lava flows. Roughly 1.6 million years ago, a nearby volcano erupted and sent four cubic miles of lava tumbling over the rim. When the lava reached the Colorado River, it cooled and formed a natural dam 2,300 feet high. The resulting reservoir took 22 years to fill and stretched all the way back to Moab, Utah. Over hundreds of thousands of years, however, the river slowly eroded the dam.

The campground at Toroweap consists of nine first-come, first-served campsites with picnic tables, fire grates, and composting toilets—but no water or electricity. If you're planning a trip to Toroweap, the main access road (BLM #109) leaves highway 389 about seven miles west of Fredonia. The unpaved road is 60 miles long and notorious for causing flat tires. High clearance and 4WD are definitely recommended.

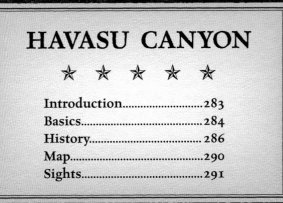

HAVASU CANYON

★ ★ ★ ★ ★

Havasu Falls

HAVASU CANYON

To GRAND CANYON visitors in the know, the word Havasu conjures up images of a remote desert paradise. Located about 35 miles west of Grand Canyon Village, Havasu Canyon is one of the most beautiful places in the Southwest. For over 700 years, it has been the home of the Havasupai, the "People of the Blue-Green Water," who derive their name from the vibrant turquoise stream that flows through the center of the canyon. Today roughly 450 Havasupai continue to live in the tiny village of Supai, which is located 2,000 feet below Grand Canyon's rim. A short distance from the village are Havasu Falls and Mooney Falls—two of the most stunning waterfalls in America.

Although Havasu Canyon only receives an average of nine inches of rain each year, a natural spring near Supai releases nearly forty million gallons of water a day. The color of the water, an unearthly blue more typical of the Caribbean than the desert Southwest, is caused by natural minerals dissolved in the water. As Havasu Creek flows down the red rock canyon, it tumbles over dozens of beautiful pools and cascades. The creek also supports a lush riparian habitat of cottonwood trees, maidenhair fern, and scarlet monkey flowers.

Is Havasu Canyon too good to be true? Almost. Due to its rugged, remote location, getting here is a bit of a challenge. Hualapai Hilltop, the jumping off point for the eight-mile hike into the canyon, is reached after a long drive along desolate roads. From the hilltop you can descend into the canyon by foot, on mule, or by helicopter. No roads lead to Supai, which is the last town in the United States where daily mail is still delivered by mule. Furthermore, all visitors to Havasu must obtain a permit before entering the canyon. To prevent overcrowding, the Havasupai limit the number of daily permits issued.

Because Havasu Canyon remains cut off from much of the outside world, the pace of life here is distinctly different. The Havasupai continue to speak their native language, horses and dogs freely roam the dirt roads, and illumination is mostly provided by the sun and the moon. All this, combined with breathtaking natural scenery, makes a visit to Havasu Canyon one of the most fascinating adventures in America.

Basic Info

For the most up-to-date info on Havasu Canyon, check the Havasupai Tribe's official website: www.havasupai-nsn.gov

Getting to Havasu

Although Havasu Canyon only lies about 35 miles west of Grand Canyon Village, it's about 200 miles away by road. The trail to the village of Supai starts at the rim of Havasu Canyon at Hualapai Hilltop. To get there from Grand Canyon Village, take I-40 to the town of Seligman, then turn onto AZ-66 heading toward Peach Springs. A little under 30 miles past Seligman (six miles east of Peach Springs), turn onto Indian Route Highway 18 and follow it roughly 60 miles to Hualapai Hilltop. From the hilltop you have three options to get to Supai:

On Foot: The trail to Supai is about eight miles long and descends 3,000 vertical feet. Plan on roughly four hours hiking down and five hours hiking up. Despite some switchbacks near the top, the majority of the trail is a moderate/easy hike. You can also arrange to have your gear carried down by mule (see below). Note: The campground is an additional two miles beyond Supai.

By Mule: Mule rides to Supai cost $75 per person one-way, $120 round-trip. A ride to the campground, located two miles past Supai, costs $95 one-way, $190 round-trip.

By Helicopter: Airwest Helicopters offers service from Hualapai Hilltop to Supai. Cost is $85 per person one-way, and flights are generally offered between 10am and 1pm. (623-516-2790, www.airwesthelicopters.com)

Permits & Fees

All visitors must have an advance reservation at either the campground or lodge prior to arrival. There's also a $35 per person entrance fee, plus a $5 per person environmental impact fee. All campers must check in and pay the fee at the tourist office in Supai, open 7am–7pm April–Oct, 8am–5pm Nov–March. One mule can also carry up to four bags weighing up to 130 pounds for the price of one rider. (928-448-2121, 928-448-2174, 928-448-2180)

Guided Tours

The following companies offer guided, multi-day tours of Havasu Canyon:
Grand Canyon Field Institute (www.grandcanyon.org/fieldinstitute)
Arizona Outback Adventures (www.aoa-adventures.com, 480-945-2881)
Wildland Trekking Company (www.wildlandtrekking.com, 800-715-4453)
Discovery Treks (www.discoverytreks.com, 888-256-8731)

Lodging

The small, two-story Havasu Lodge in Supai offers 24 motel-style rooms that sleep up to four. All rooms have air conditioning and private bathrooms, but no telephones or TV. Be aware that May through October is peak tourist season, and the lodge is often booked months in advance. Rates: $145 per room/per night, up to four people per room. (928-448-2201)

Camping

A large 200-person campground, located two miles north of Supai near Havasu Falls, is open year-round. Campsites are located on either side of Havasu Stream, and composting toilets were recently installed. A hand pump near the head of the campground provides drinking water. Reservations are generally easy to come by, except during peak summer season or on busy holiday weekends. Cost: $17 per person/per night. (928-448-2141, 928-448-2121)

Food & Dining

There's only one restaurant in Supai: the Tribal Cafe, which serves cafeteria-style fast food (try the Indian Taco). Hours vary, but the cafe is generally open 6am–6pm in the summer, 8am–5pm in the winter (928-448-2981). There's also a small grocery store across from the cafe that sells basic goods. A few Havasu families also run micro-stores and restaurants out of their homes (look for the signs as you stroll through town).

Lodging Near Hualapai Hilltop

Driving to Hualapai Hilltop from Grand Canyon Village or any other nearby city takes several hours, and after a long drive the last thing you'll want to do is start a long journey into Havasu Canyon. A better option is to spend the night at one of the hotels located along AZ-66 and start out early in the morning. This is especially true in the summer, when morning shade provides relief from the sun.

GRAND CANYON CAVERNS INN

This basic 48-room motel, located along an empty stretch of highway, offers the closest lodging to Hualapai Hilltop.
Rates: $85–$95 (928-422-3223, www.gccaverns.com)

HUALAPAI LODGE

This modern 60-room hotel, located in the small town of Peach Springs, is definitely a step up from Grand Canyon Caverns Inn, but you'll have to drive a few extra miles to reach Hualapai Hilltop.
Rates: $100-130. (928-769-2636, www.grandcanyonwest.com)

HISTORY

GENETIC EVIDENCE INDICATES the Havasupai are descended from the first wave of human migrants to enter North America roughly 20,000 years ago. The Havasupai refer to themselves as *Havsuw 'Baaja* ("People of the Blue-Green Water"), and Havasupai creation myths speak of a time when Coyote and other animal gods imparted their wisdom to the tribe, thus establishing their basic customs and rituals. Archaeological evidence indicates that Havasu Canyon has been occupied for at least 700 years.

In the summer, the Havasupai tended gardens of beans, corn, and squash. Their irrigation techniques, possibly imported from Mexico, were among the most advanced in the Southwest. In addition to Havasu Canyon, they farmed several side canyons along Grand Canyon's South Rim, including Indian Gardens below present-day Grand Canyon Village. Dozens of wild plants such as agave and pinyon pine also provided additional food.

Although Havasu Canyon was home to the tribe's most prominent village, their territory covered a vast area along much of the South Rim. In the winter, when the sun only shines in Havasu Canyon for a few hours each day, the tribe moved to the open plateaus along the South Rim. Snow provided a steady source of water, firewood was abundant, and rabbit and deer supplemented their diet.

Daily life revolved around farming, food gathering, hunting, cooking, tool-making, and socializing. Social conformity was extremely important, and those who did not follow traditional Havasupai ways were publicly shamed and ostracized. Women were often treated as property, and polygamy was sometimes practiced by high status males. But there was no formal marriage ceremony. After a single woman's family had been given sufficient gifts by a suitor, the woman and man were considered "married."

Traditional Havasupai dwellings consisted of earth-covered conical huts with dirt floors. Clothes, moccasins, and blankets were crafted from animal hides, and women often decorated themselves with face paint and jewelry. Important ceremonies also featured elaborate costumes and body paint.

The Havasupai had friendly relations with the nearby Hopi and Navajo, and the tribes often gathered at annual celebrations that involved feasting, dancing, and gambling. During these gatherings, the Havasupai traded vegetables and buckskin for jewelry and blankets. But not all nearby tribes had friendly relations with the Havasupai. The Yavapai and Paiute occasionally carried out violent raids on Havasu Canyon. To defend their territory, the Havasupai retreated to high cliffs where they could shoot arrows poisoned with toxic liquids extracted from plants and scorpions. Heavy rocks were also rolled down on the invaders.

Following the arrival of the Spanish in North America, the Havasupai indirectly acquired horses and added melons, peaches, and pears to their gardens. But due to their remote location, they had little direct contact with the Spaniards, and their lifestyle was far less impacted than those of other tribes.

In the mid-1800s, white miners and ranchers began arriving in northern Arizona. Land conflicts became common, and in 1882 the federal government placed the tribe on a reservation in Havasu Canyon less than a square mile in size. A separate reservation was set up for the Hualapai ("Pine Tree People") on the rim. Forced onto separate reservations, the Havasupai and Hualapai became two distinct tribes, although previously they may have considered themselves part of the same tribe. The Havasupai were also denied access to their traditional winter hunting grounds on the rim. This was a devastating blow to the Havasupai. They now found themselves confined to a tiny reservation with barely enough farming area to feed themselves year-round. Previously unknown European diseases also ravaged the Havasupai, and their population fell precipitously.

Meanwhile, as more and more manufactured goods trickled into the region, the Havasupai abandoned many of their traditional ways. Cotton shirts replaced animal skins, rifles replaced bows and arrows, and pottery was completely abandoned. But despite the changes, the Havasupai held on to their culture better than most other tribes. In the 1930s, an anthropologist visiting Supai remarked that it was "the only spot in the United States where native culture has remained in anything like its pristine condition." But as the decades wore on, the Havasupai continued to suffer. Alcohol and diabetes were soon added to the tribe's growing list of problems. The loss of land, harsh living conditions, and cultural upheaval had left many Havasupai angry and demoralized.

Throughout much of the 20th century, the tribe waged a long-shot legal battle to reclaim much of their former territory. They were up against powerful forces. Their former territory now belonged to Grand Canyon National Park, and both the park service and environmental organizations like the Sierra Club fought to keep the land protected in federal hands. The Havasupai, who had sustainably interacted with their environment for centuries, were stunned when they were told to stay off the land so that plants and animals could be protected.

Undeterred, the Havasupai continued to press their case. A turning point came in 1973, when they met with Arizona senator Barry Goldwater, who offered his support. Two years later, on January 4, 1975, over 250,000 acres were returned to the Havasupai. In addition to land on the rim, the tribe regained control of the area below Havasu Falls, which had been operated as a national park campground. Seeking to alleviate the poverty that had plagued them for decades, the Havasupai took full control of Havasu Canyon's tourist operations.

Today tourism generates $2.5 million annually for the tribe. And though modernization has come to Supai in the form of electricity, telephones, and the internet, the pace of life remains distinctly different. Any suggestions to build a modern road into the canyon have always been rejected, and today the Havasupai boast the highest percentage of native speakers of any tribe in the U.S.

Wii Gl'iiva

These prominent rock spires guard the northern entrance to Havasu Canyon and are considered sacred by the Havasupai. Legend states that when the rocks fall, the walls of Havasu Canyon will close and the tribe will be no more.

Flooding in Havasu

FLOODING IS A fact of life in Havasu Canyon, which experiences a flood on average every three years. The canyon drains a watershed encompassing nearly 3,000 square miles, and runoff from thunderstorms funnels into Havasu Canyon with astonishing speed. Most floods are minor and merely a nuisance. But every few years a massive thunderstorm dumps enormous quantities of rain in a remarkably short period of time. When this happens, the consequences for Havasu Canyon are severe.

In 1900 a woman named Flora Gregg Iliff was teaching in Havasu Canyon when she experienced a flash flood first-hand. Her terrifying account is recorded in her book *People of the Blue* Water: "With startling suddenness, a full-grown river, boiling with sand and debris, leaped over the east wall with a force that shot it far out into the canyon ... Nothing could stand against that roaring waterfall. It hurled a boulder over the rim, spun it crazily and smashed it on the ground with an impact that shook the canyon." During the flood, the Havasupai did what they have always done: retreat to the high cliffs surrounding the canyon and wait for the waters to subside. The tribe also stored a year's worth of food in the cliffs above Supai in case flooding destroyed their crops.

In January 1910 the largest flood in recorded history tore through Havasu Canyon, peaking at an estimated 35,000 cubic feet per second—1,000 times greater than Havasu Creek's normal flow. Every building in Supai was destroyed. Fortunately the flood occurred in winter, when most of the tribe was living on the rim, and many lives were spared. In 1990 the second largest flood in recorded history tore through Havasu Canyon, peaking at roughly 20,000 cfs. Three years later, another flood maxed out at roughly 10,000 cfs. Flooding can occur in both winter and summer, but nearly 80 percent of historical Havasu Creek floods have occurred during or immediately following El Niño years.

More recently, in August 2008, a flash flood made headlines when it dramatically reshaped Havasu's famous waterfalls. The flood tore out a new streambed downstream of Supai, diverting the creek away from Navajo Falls (previously the first large waterfall encountered below Supai) and creating two new waterfalls. Remarkably, the 2008 flood was estimated at only 6,000 cubic feet per second, making it the 17th smallest flood in recorded history. But its power was severe. According to one witness in the campground, "All kinds of debris went rushing by including an outhouse, tents, water toys, cottonwood trees and boulders." Fortunately, thanks to many Havasupai First Responders, there were no casualties in the campground and residents of Supai were unharmed. Type "Havasu Flood 2008" into YouTube to find some dramatic video footage taken by visitors during the flood.

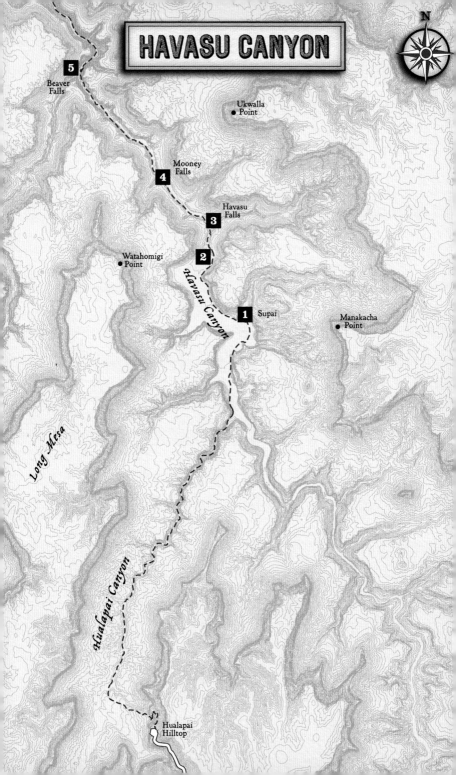

1 Supai Village

This small village, home to roughly 450 full-time residents, is the permanent home of the Havasupai Tribe. If you're arriving on foot, you'll reach Supai after twisting and turning through Havasu's narrow upper canyons. After descending into a large, open canyon floor, you'll follow a series of dusty dirt roads until you reach the tourist office, where all visitors must check in. Continue down the street to reach "downtown" Supai, home to the village cafe, market, post office, community center, and K-8 school (when the children reach high school they attend a boarding school outside the canyon). The Supai lodge, a Christian church, and a Mormon church are also located nearby. Follow the main road north of the majestic *Wii Gl'iiva* and soon the road will turn into a trail that heads down to Havasu's famous waterfalls and the campground.

Some visitors are dismayed by what they find in Supai. Hoping to experience a hidden paradise "uncorrupted" by the modern world, they instead find modest homes topped with satellite dishes and a helicopter dropping off supplies. The Havasupai are proud of their ancient culture and continue to speak their native tongue, but they have eagerly embraced many aspects of the modern world. Some visitors are also surprised by the run-down condition of some parts of town. But remember that living in a remote, isolated canyon presents many challenges. (You can't just run to the hardware store whenever something breaks.) As you walk through Supai, remind yourself that you are a guest of the Havasupai and be respectful of their home.

2 New Waterfalls

In August 2008 a flash flood tore through Havasu Canyon, completely reshaping the scenery between Supai and Havasu Falls. The flood ripped out vegetation, carved out an entirely new watercourse, and created two "new" waterfalls. (In fact, the uppermost falls was called "Fifty-Foot Falls" until a flash flood buried it in sediment sometime around 1940. The 2008 flood simply re-exposed the old waterfall.) As of this writing, the new waterfalls did not have official names. Until the tribe officially names them, some people are calling the waterfalls "Old" Fifty-Foot Falls (right) and Rock Falls (above). "Old" Fifty-Foot Falls is now about 70 feet high, and Rock Falls is about 30 feet high. Notice the vast stretch of dead trees on the ridge above Rock Falls. Prior to 2008, Havasu Creek supported a vast riparian habitat along the ridge. Although the old habitat died after the water shifted course, new habitat is slowly forming along the banks of the new creek.

Havasu Creek's new waterway completely bypasses Navajo Falls, a 75-foot waterfall that was once considered one of the canyon's prettiest sights. It is frequently claimed that Navajo Falls was destroyed by the 2008 flood, but the waterfall's extensive travertine structure remains intact, creating, in effect, a "fossilized" waterfall. Although impossible to see from the trail, Navajo Falls is located downstream of Rock Falls beyond the river's western bank. Although the loss of Navajo Falls is tragic, it is part of the natural cycle of destruction and regeneration that has shaped Havasu Canyon for thousands of years. And besides, the new waterfalls sure look pretty.

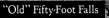
"Old" Fifty-Foot Falls

3 Havasu Falls

Havasu Falls, the star attraction of Havasu Canyon, is located roughly half a mile past the new waterfalls that formed in 2008. As the trail drops down along the sheer western wall of Havasu Canyon, the roar of the falls grows louder. Suddenly, Havasu Falls appears on your right. At this point you're at eye level with the top of the 90-foot falls. Continue down the trail to reach several well-trodden side trails that lead to a beach area shaded by cottonwood trees. Although often crowded in summer, the beach is without question one of the most spectacular swimming holes in America.

A century ago, Havasu Falls looked completely different. Back then the water tumbled over the cliff in a 200-foot wide curtain of water, and it was called Bridal Veil Falls. In 1910 a flash flood roared through Havasu Canyon and knocked out a large notch in the cliff. Suddenly, the water was channeled into a much narrower—and much more spectacular—waterfall. Other flash floods have been far less kind. In 1993 a flash flood destroyed several beautiful travertine terraces at the base of the falls that formed a series of cascading pools. Then, during the flood of 2008, the beautiful "apron" that defined the falls for decades was destroyed. The flood knocked out a small notch in the apron, creating a narrow chute that forms a far less dramatic waterfall. But take a look at the numerous travertine formations on either side of the falls. These are the prehistoric remnants of older versions of Havasu Falls—a potent reminder that the waterfall has been naturally changing shape for thousands of years.

Why is the Water in Havasu Blue?

EVEN WITHOUT ITS colorful, spring-fed creek, Havasu Canyon would still be a remarkable destination. But the vibrant blue water, contrasted with striking red rocks, gives the canyon an otherworldly beauty. What makes the water so blue? The answer is chemistry. Specifically, dissolved calcium carbonate and magnesium that occur naturally in Havasu Creek.

The process starts when rain falls on the surrounding plateaus and water seeps into the ground. Over thousands of years, the water slowly trickles through Grand Canyon's rock layers, dissolving rocks and picking up minerals along the way. Eventually the water reaches the deep underground aquifers that feed Havasu Springs. (Carbon dating indicates that the water flowing from Havasu Springs is over 11,000 years old). The water in Havasu Springs is saturated with calcium and bicarbonate (dissolved from limestone) and magnesium (which gives the water its brilliant blue tint). As the water enters the canyon, the sudden drop in pressure and increase in temperature causes solid calcium carbonate to precipitate out of the water. The calcium carbonate ultimately forms shiny layers of travertine along the creekbed, which further reflect the blue-tinted water. As the creek flows down the canyon, massive quantities of travertine are deposited—by some measures up to 70,000 pounds *each day*. This, in turn, leads to another fascinating phenomenon: as calcium bicarbonate precipitates out of the water, the relative saturation of magnesium increases. Thus the water in Havasu Creek gets bluer and bluer the farther downstream it flows!

4 Mooney Falls

At 196 feet, Mooney Falls is the tallest waterfall in Havasu Canyon. To get there, follow the main trail one mile past Havasu Falls to a stunning overlook at the end of the campground. The path to the base of the falls is an Indiana Jones-style adventure that involves scrambling through a tunnel carved by 19th century miners, followed by a slippery descent down a rickety ladder.

The Havasupai call this waterfall "Mother of the Waters," and they consider it their most sacred waterfall. The name Mooney Falls comes from a tragic accident that occurred here in 1880. In that year, a group of American prospectors entered Havasu Canyon looking for gold. When they reached this waterfall they could go no farther, and a man named Daniel Mooney volunteered to be lowered down by rope. But shortly after Mooney began his descent, the rope became stuck in a jagged crevice. As his friends struggled with the rope, it began to fray. Suddenly, the rope snapped, and Mooney fell to his death. Unable to reach Mooney's body, the prospectors abandoned their search and went home. Ten months later they returned and built a ladder to the base of the falls, but by that point Mooney's body had been encrusted in a fresh layer of travertine.

A few decades later, Mooney Falls was taken from the Havasupai by the federal government, and a private company attempted to build a hydro-electric plant here. But before the power plant was completed, a flash flood tore through the canyon, destroying the machinery and bankrupting the company. In 1975 the government returned the waterfall to the Havasupai tribe.

5 Below Mooney Falls

Below Mooney Falls a rugged trail continues down Havasu Canyon all the way to the Colorado River. Along the way the trail passes through some of Havasu Canyon's most beautiful scenery. The water gets bluer. The vegetation gets lusher. Cascading pools are scattered between leafy expanses of wild grapes. As you hike further downstream the crowds thin out, and soon it will feel like you have Havasu Canyon all to yourself.

It's eight rugged miles from Mooney Falls to the Colorado River, which is well beyond the limits of most day hikers. The most popular destination is Beaver Falls, located roughly four miles beyond the base of Mooney Falls at the conflux of Havasu Canyon and Beaver Canyon. A series of cascading pools, Beaver Falls offers amazing scenery and divine swimming opportunities. In my opinion, it's one of the highlights of Havasu Canyon. But there's a catch. The trail below Mooney Falls is gorgeous, but it becomes harder to follow the further downstream you go. A trip to Beaver Falls involves multiple river crossings and steep scrambles involving wobbly ladders and ropes. Experienced hikers with good trail finding skills can probably figure it out, but out-of-shape hikers uncomfortable with heights and river crossings should definitely avoid the long hike to Beaver Falls. That said, if you've made it to the base of Mooney Falls, it's definitely worth following the trail for as long as you feel comfortable. There's plenty of gorgeous scenery to be enjoyed along the way.

Beaver Falls

Route 66

This classic American highway was the first major route between Chicago and Los Angeles. Completed in 1926, the 2,448-mile roadway served as the primary path for Dust Bowl migrants heading west in the 1930s. It was later made famous by the Bobby Troup song "(Get Your Kicks on) Route 66," which was covered by Nat King Cole, Perry Como and Chuck Berry. By the 1960s, Route 66 had become a romantic symbol of American automobile freedom, but it fell on hard times following the construction of the Interstate Highway System. As motorists abandoned the old two-lane highway for the speedier Interstate, roadside mom-and-pop businesses closed down by the thousands. By 1985 Route 66 was officially removed from the U.S. Highway System.

But nostalgia for an American Icon dies hard, and in recent years Route 66 has experienced something of a revival. Although much of the original highway was swallowed up by Interstate 40 near Grand Canyon, classic stretches of Route 66 remain. Downtown Williams celebrates its Route 66 heritage through retro diners and coffee shops, but if you're looking for the "authentic" experience head 43 miles west to the town of Seligman. The real-life inspiration for the town of Radiator Springs in the Pixar movie *Cars*, Seligman is a shadow of its former self, yet still retains a faded 50s-era charm. Its most famous roadside restaurant, Delgadillo's Snow Cap Drive-In, has been serving burgers, fries and practical jokes since 1953. From Seligman, Route 66 arcs north through the desert for 85 miles before rejoining with Interstate 40 at Kingman.

Grand Canyon West

Owned and operated by the Hualapai Tribe (p.61), Grand Canyon West encompasses 108 miles along Grand Canyon's southwest rim. Although not part of the national park, its views are breathtaking nonetheless. Grand Canyon West is located 250 miles (5 hours driving) from Grand Canyon National Park's South Rim. From Las Vegas it's just 125 miles (2.5 hours driving), making it a popular destination for day-tripping tourists wanting to catch a glimpse of Grand Canyon. In addition to scenic viewpoints, Grand Canyon West offers horseback rides, helicopter tours and rafting day trips along the Colorado River. Its most famous attraction, however, is the Grand Canyon Skywalk (above). This semi-circular bridge, which juts out 70 feet from the Canyon's edge, features a glass floor that offers visitors dramatic views 3,600 feet down to the Colorado River. When the Skywalk opened in 2007, astronaut Buzz Aldrin was the first person to walk across it publicly. He was followed by John Bennet Harrington, the first Native American in space.

To enter Grand Canyon West, you'll need to purchase the "Hualapai Legacy Package" ($30 per person), which provides basic entry plus access to viewpoints, cultural activities, live performances and a wagon ride. Horseback tours, helicopter rides and rafting trips all require an additional fee. To walk on the Skywalk, you'll need to purchase the "Legacy Gold Package" ($71 per person), which is essentially a Legacy Package with the Skywalk plus a meal. Overnight accommodations are also available. (888-868-9378, www.grandcanyonwest.com)

The Best of the Best

For photos, hotel info and guidebook updates
visit www.jameskaiser.com